Fall from Grace

Nathan Daniels

authorHOUSE

AuthorHouse™ UK Ltd.
1663 Liberty Drive
Bloomington, IN 47403 USA
www.authorhouse.co.uk
Phone: 0800.197.4150

© *2014 Nathan Daniels. All rights reserved.*

No part of this book may be reproduced, stored in a retrieval system, or transmitted by any means without the written permission of the author.

Published by AuthorHouse 09/01/2014

ISBN: 978-1-4918-9274-9 (sc)
ISBN: 978-1-4969-8925-3 (hc)
ISBN: 978-1-4969-8926-0 (e)

Any people depicted in stock imagery provided by Thinkstock are models, and such images are being used for illustrative purposes only. Certain stock imagery © Thinkstock.

This book is printed on acid-free paper.

Because of the dynamic nature of the Internet, any web addresses or links contained in this book may have changed since publication and may no longer be valid. The views expressed in this work are solely those of the author and do not necessarily reflect the views of the publisher, and the publisher hereby disclaims any responsibility for them.

The good old thank you page

I have been in way to many institutions to name them all, but they all played a part in me getting clean and healthy.

The real thanks goes out to all the people close to me, my mother, father and sister, who without them, Im sure I would have met my untimely death on the streets. To the Green Family for always having my back, I'll never forget it. To my beautiful daughter, daddy's litle angel. Love you with everything my baby. To Marna for bringing Kayla into the world. Lastly to all the individuals that stood by me, taught me lessons, gave me love, made me smile when I wanted to cry and to those who showed me that life can be beautiful once again.

Prologue

Icy winter rain whips my face. Suddenly everything becomes real. I cry.

What's going on? Where did it all go so fucking wrong? I can't stop, no matter what. I've been to the best rehabs, had the best counselors and still it won't stop. The truth is I don't think I want it to stop. To some extent I do don't get me wrong, I want the chaos to end and the pain to subside but I can't make the decision to actually end it.

Memories float in of the first time I used ecstasy, heroin and meth. The pleasure that filled my body… There has been nothing in this world so far that can compare. Nothing has even come close. I can't stop, I won't stop. Fuck it. I don't want to stop.

I've been on the streets of Sea Point for a week or two now. Cape winters are so different to our Jozi winters. It's rainy, windy and cold all at the same time. Finding shelter in Sea Point is hard unless you're willing to bunk with a nasty smelling hobo. All the prime spots are taken. There's a weird little cove on the shore line. I think it's in the vicinity of Green Point. It does the trick to cover the wind and the rain but not the cold and it's riddled with fucking crabs.

I steal whenever I can, to eat and keep my addiction running at full tilt. I drink a really cheap red wine. Occasionally, when I'm lucky, I drink Russian Bear Vodka but this drink always comes after the smack and smokes.

I wonder how long it's going to take till I die, because that's for certain. The winter is brutal, the rocks I sleep on, uncomfortable, the drugs I use, hard. Surely one of these things will kill me.

Nathan Daniels

Where did it all go wrong? Was it the heroin that did this or the weed right at the start? Was it because I swore on my life even though I was lying? Was it because I'm cursed? These questions can't be answered by any mortal. I need to talk to God. When I die I'm going to hell, so I don't know when I'll ever talk to our maker. My adopted family doesn't care anymore. If I die, would they really care? Would they cry at my funeral while some odd Rabbi I've never met say things I don't understand or care about? Would he go on to say what a shame it was to see such a young life fall away? Would he say what a caring loving boy I was? Would he say I'd be missed by all who knew me? What a bunch of crap! I don't care for anyone but myself. All I've done is to rage havoc across my family ties. My dad once said I'm an embarrassment. So fuck everyone.

I lie solidly awake on my rock solid bed, holding the little bag of heroin tight so that it doesn't get wet or cold. I sip the last of the vodka out the bottle. I still have a joint to smoke, so at least I'll sleep tonight. But I know what comes tomorrow. Rain, wind, cold and the worst alcohol and heroin withdrawals you could imagine. Not to mention my sore back from this cardboard I sleep on. I hope I die, I hope that I get snuffed out by some mysterious force.

I don't want to live anymore. I mean ... really ... what's the point of living this fucking existence, it's pointless. Well maybe I can help some West African to feed his family or maybe I will fund a small war. Who knows where my money will go once it's been handed over to those Nigerians. What I'm trying to say is that it's demeaning and humiliating to be a slave to that little fucking bag of off-white powder. Only an addict knows the power of that little bag of white substance. I swear to you, when the sweating and cramping starts, be it from alcohol, pharmaceuticals, or anything I'm hooked on at the time, I will do anything in my power to get that next bag, line or pill. Yes is the answers to that question you just thought of. Yes, ANYTHING!!!

Chapter 1

My first memory is warm, cozy and comfortable. I wake up to the soothing touch of my dear nanny. She says: 'Nathan*, wake up, it's time for school.' She says it in her mixed accent of Zulu and English. 'But Rose*, it's still dark', I say while sitting up in my oversized bed. 'Its okay, Boy. The sun is rising.' She says this while helping me up. 'Nathan, your bath is waiting for you. You don't want the water to get cold, do you?' 'No', I say, still struggling to open my eyes. 'So then jump up and let's get going.'

She's very nice. I love Rose. She comes from Natal. She's short, plump and has an infectious smile. Her teeth are so white I think she brushes them with bleach or something. Rose is always around. Like a shadow, she's always there if I need anything. She always comes through for me. Like a mom.

I stumble out of my oversized room onto the cold white tiles, making my way to my bathroom, where steam rises out the tub. I really love Rose. I strip out my phi's and hop into the searing hot water. It's beautiful, just like the sky I can see through the sky light. I lie back and take in the heat. Winter in South Africa can be very cold you know?

I often wake up in the morning and there's frost on the grass. When you exhale, fog comes out of your mouth and the temperature in the car usually reads below five degrees on the way to school. It's strange because when I lie here and I look at the baby blue sky, it looks nice, welcoming and warm. Yet I've been on this earth long enough to know that it's freezing out there.

Rose rushes into the bathroom. 'Have you washed yourself young man?' 'No Rose. I'm so tired I can't do it.' 'Come on', she says, picking up the soap and sponge. She gives me a thorough rub down and hoists me out the water into a warm puffy towel. 'We need to get you ready and dressed so you don't miss your lift.' We walk back into my room. I run and jump under the covers of my still slightly warm bed, trying to savor that nice morning feeling.

'Come on Nathan, we must hurry.' I stammer out again with a fat lip. My freshly ironed uniform sits on a hanger awaiting its body. Rose dresses me fast. 'Quickly Boy, get to the kitchen and eat your breakfast.' I run up the stairs, past the TV-room, past the lounge, past the atrium and the front door. I make a sharp left before the dining room and enter the huge kitchen. There sits a plate of eggs setting off streams of sunlight in the sun that flows through the window. I love Rose. She magically makes eggs appear, while bathing and dressing me. She's a wonderful lady, old Rose.

I gulp the eggs down with salt and tomato sauce. Just as I finish my lovely breakfast, my dad walks into the kitchen with his briefcase and bleached white dental suit. Seems people in this house like to use bleach a lot. He kisses my head, grabs his little lunch bag and walks out for a hard day's work. I love my daddy also.

Dr Lancaster as he prefers to be called is a dentist. By dentists' standards I believe him to be successful. He has his own practice, with a whole bunch of dentists working for him. He seems to make some serious money shown by the way we live, because we live really well. I mean our house was in one of those House & Home books, decorated by a very serious decorator. Our cars were always big, German and expensive. Our holidays were tropical and we even had a house in Portugal.

So by all means Jeff Lancaster was successful. When I look back now, he was a good dad. I believe that, besides spending time with their kids, fathers display their love by how hard they work. Obviously this translates into supporting the family. *Note to self: Supporting the family is love, isn't it?*

We used to go fishing and on family outings on Sundays, we ate dinner together every evening. Yes, on the whole, Jeff was a good old man.

The Daimler's hooter honks outside our gate, I run to kiss my mom, and then I run back upstairs. I'm greeted by Rose holding my school bag. We walk down the long drive way. Then the gate magically opens another one of Saint Rose's tricks. I step into the Daimler. I love you Rose.

Chapter 2

I scurry around Jan Smuts Airport in a nervous rage, fearful of what lies ahead. The beige linoleum floor is slippery with cheap, greasy wax, but that's the last thing on my mind. My father is a middle aged man who looks like he's pushing sixty. He tries to control everything around him, including the family's emotions.

'Don't worry guys; this is going to be amazing. It's a brand new start, Nathan. Have you ever been on a bus or a train?' My father speaks with a confidence so weak and fake that even I can see he's lying to himself. 'We don't have a pool in Australia but we do have the sea in our back yard. You'll love the beach Cara. You can tan and swim whenever you want.'

'Dad, what if we don't like it there?' I ask timidly. He says 'Two years is all I'm asking for. Let's give it a good go, and after two years, if you still want to come back, then we will.'

His answer fails miserably as we all stand broken and torn. We're a miserable bunch. Then comes the call to board the plane to hell. It starts as we walk down the ramp. Our hopeless, powerless tears again well. I scream, sob and moan to the point that my nose starts to bleed. This is a bad move. I resent it. I hate my father deeply for the decision he's imposed on us. Fuck you Dad.

'You're excited about the new start, Boy?' he asks as if this is the greatest decision he's ever made. 'Sort of,' I respond, shaking my head.

'There's lots of cool stuff to do in Sydney, you know.' Another one of his genius lines, I say to myself. 'You've got the beach, buses, trains and, most importantly, freedom and safety.' 'Sounds great', I mumble sarcastically.

My mother looks back at me with her *behave yourself* eyes, as if to say, be nice to your father, he is trying to make our lives better.

Fuck both of them for trying to gang up on me. I'm unhappy and I'll stay that way for as long as I like.

As we board the plane that familiar smell of sweat, recycled earphones and tears drifts into my nostrils. I used to love airplanes and airports. I no longer do. This emigration has burned pain into my life. All my true friends will forget me. The fabulous life I once had is now a distant memory, slowly fading with each step I take towards Sydney. My house I grew up in, the only house I've ever known

is gone. Why can't I understand?

I wonder why we're always in economy class. Cramped seats with babies crying and miniature bottles of whiskey that a midget wouldn't appreciate. I wander upstairs to see first class. I'm stunned by the size of the chairs. Some of my friends' beds aren't that big. This sucks. My father should've got us decent seats. We're going to hell, and we could have done it in style. Fuck you Dad. 'Thanks for the great seats Dad, you're a legend,' I say under my breath as I walk back to my matchbox seat. 'What, Boy?' 'Nothing, Dad.'

There's a fat man sitting in front of me. He smells like beer and those shitty roasted nuts. This is going to suck, and his seat hasn't even started to lean back. Why do they have these colours on planes? The navy seats show all the marks from the babies that have thrown up on them. The brown and navy chequered carpet looks cheap and easy to replace. The sides are fake plastic grey. On close inspection, one sees small cracks. Not to mention the windows. I need to get off this death trap.

I lament like a maniac: 'Dad, can't we move up stairs?'

Or, even better…, right off the plane would be great. I know this is an ill-advised idea.

'Relax, everything is going to be fine, boy', he retorts. Rummaging in his man bag, he pulls out a blister pack of tablets. 'Here… take this sleeping pill.'

I gulp the pill down with excitement. That's what I need, sleep. But it doesn't come. I wonder what Australia is going to be like – Lonely? Fun?

Freedom? *Note to self: Fuck freedom. I want my life back.*

'Dad, what movies are they playing? I can't see the TV.'

'The film hasn't started yet. Go to sleep.'

'Dad, I'm not tired', I reply. Then the same thought crosses my mind, and I dare say: 'DAD, WHY ARE YOU DOING THIS TO US!?!'

'Control yourself.'

'I'm sorry, Dad. I'll behave. Please can we get off the plane? Please, Daddy, please?'

After about an hour of asking questions, irritating my sister and mother, and sending my dad into an anxious fit, something happens. Something profound comes about. I try to lift my feet but they won't move easily. My fingers tingle, and my heart slows down. What is going on here?

'Dad, I feel weird, my toes won't move.'

'Talk and walk up and down the plane to get the blood flowing', he says like a true medical professional, even though he's only a dentist.

I stand and my head spins. Then it happens – the thing that makes me different to *normal people*. I stumble to the back. The feeling is unbelievable; my dull reality is banished. The plane is wonderful, the carpets are soft, and the chairs are comfortable and so spacious. It's like I'm in a small hotel with no walls. I know this feeling.

I'm eleven years old. As per usual, Mom and Dad go out on a Saturday night for dinner with friends. They leave me and my friends with Rose. I must explain I was a seriously a naughty kid. I don't know why things that were wrong always pulled me in. If I had a choice to do something, my decision-making process got corrupted or was drawn towards the negative. The more I learn about myself, the more I see that most of my decision-making was based on changing feelings, escaping feelings or the instant grat of pleasure.

This particular evening was the normal routine: Skating on the patio, grinding the steps or the swimming pool pole, playing Metallica, Nirvana or Offspring, and just doing our thing. Can't remember where the notion came from, maybe it was a learnt behaviour, but the idea bounced to my mind that we should drink my dad's alcohol. So, in true fashion to how the older gents drank, we took the crystal whiskey glasses, and added ice. From what I could gather at that tender age, a single meant one finger and a double meant two fingers. I specifically remember my dad holding two fingers horizontally on the glass and pouring the beautiful golden liquid till it reached his fingers. So, wanting to be like the older blokes, I poured a double. It smelt pretty bad but there must have been a reason why they drank this foul smelling liquid. I took my first sip. Instantly, my face wrinkled up, and shivers spread through my body. The burning sensation that alcohol of this strength creates was too much to bear, so I tried my hardest to act like it wasn't at all that bad. The other two boys followed suit.

Something that I will probably never forget happened that night: The soothing, ultra pleasurable feeling of being tipsy reared its ugly but beautiful head in my young life. To this day I still feel the relief of that first drink - that ultimate careless, that reckless abandonment of the self.

To end off this experience, we went from skating and falling over the place to sitting in my parents' garden. We sat in the sprinkler, drunk and filled with laughter. I still wonder to this day whether the two guys who drank with me had the same awe inspiring experience I had. Probably not. This is what makes me different.

I hope I land up feeling like I did that night in the garden. That was brilliant. This oversized thimble of a bathroom is making me feel sick, but it's sweet because I feel fucking phenomenal. 'Help! I can't open the door!' I bang on the door. My screams are muffled by the pill. Dizziness comes and I need to vomit. Should I push the button to call someone to come help me? The flushing of the toilet always scares me, like if someone flushed while I was still on it I would get sucked out.

Click, the door opens. That was heavy shit.

I can't find my seat. I'm totally lost in business class. I look around like a kid at preschool searching for comfort and security. A pretty hostess comes up to me.

'Are you lost Little Guy?'

'I'mm srot of lstah… evedffrythiheng ldfgoofks the sagfgtme,' I reply, my words are coming and I feel like a Japanese tourist.

She must think I'm a bit retarded, because she says, 'Its okay young man, we'll find your family.'

She ushers me back to economy class. I see my dad's balding from a distance. I mumble and point at the black hair with grey streaks through it.

'Nathan! Where have you been? We started getting worried. 'Where the hell am I going to go, Jeff? 'We're on a plane I can't exactly leave or get off. Believe me, if I could, I would've been gone a long time ago.'

I crawl back into my sardine can of a seat. The anger is building; the glorious feeling of oblivion is fading. I want to ask my dad for more, but I know he won't hand it over. Bang, that fucking food trolley hits my elbow, these fucking hostesses hate me or hate Jews or hate small people or even more likely, all of the above. There is however that little bit of excitement you get when the food trolley is getting closer and you have to play the lottery of what you're going to have. I'm very impulsive, I like to make decisions right there and then, I can't seem to make decisions based on future planning.

'Chicken, beef or fish?'

I'm one of those people who actually like airplane food, the small foil container is so exciting, like opening a lucky packet. The same with hospital food but that's a whole different story. We'll get to that at a later date.

My dad says 'Fish please', my mom says 'Beef please'. Cara, my sister, is fast asleep. I say 'Chicken please'. I know the way this family works: My dad didn't want the fish. My mom didn't want the beef. It must be a Jewish thing, because as the meal goes on they both stretch into each other's meals and mine just to make sure that they taste everything. I'm left with a tiny piece of chicken, half the fish and most of the beef, one small potato and some gross green veggies, one cracker, half the cheese and a few crumbs of a roll. Oh yeah! And that revolting apple juice my mom ordered for me.

'You know, Coke makes him hyper-active,' my mom trustingly tells the hostess.

Why don't you tell her my life story, mom? The fat man in front of me is snoring. His obesity is blocking the TV so I can barely see the movie. I need sleep. Ten hours left. I watch the sun set at 33 000 feet. It's quite beautiful, but not enough to make me feel good. My eyes begin to close and light slowly fades to dark. I feel peaceful.

I'm lost. I am running around on a beach. The fear is paralyzing. Where is everyone? I scream, but nothing comes out. Where am I? Where is my dad? Dad, I need you, please find me.

'WAKE up Boy,' says my dad, nudging me softly. 'We're landing in half an hour. Go wash your face and brush your teeth. 'Please don't leave me,' I plead, hugging him.

'Everything's going to be OK,' he reassures me with a fatherly pat on the back.

A tear rolls down my cheek; I wipe it off without anyone seeing it. My sister is bobbing her head to her Walkman. Warren G, I suspect is the culprit of her trying to look hardcore. Whatever.

The reality of my situation sets in again as I'm getting up. My body shakes. The pain is horrible. Shut it out Nathan. I approach those hideous toilets again and ask the hostess for a can of Coke. I take the can and push the door open. I look in the mirror. There are black rings under my eyes from the lack of peaceful sleep. I don't like what I see. I don't think I ever have liked myself. This fat, ugly child that no-one wants. I brush my teeth because I know my father is going to do his dental inspection when I return to my seat. I wash my face and leave the bathroom, draining the remains of the baby Coke. WHY DAD?

My feet are swollen and sore. My hands hurt. I'm going to complain to him till we land, he deserves it. I slump back into the seat. It's time to do the work of a trusty little brother, so I poke my sister in the face and giggle.

She says, 'Nathan, I'm not in the mood for your crap.'

'Too bad, we still got forty minutes and I know you're not going anywhere.' I attempt to tickle her, but she smacks me. Not so funny. I smack her back. She's so easy to mess with. 'Dad, Cara hit me.'

'Cara, leave your brother alone.' She shakes her head and puts her ear phones back on.

'Attention ladies and gentlemen, we're beginning our descent into Sydney International Airport. Please fasten your seat belts and make sure your chair and stowaway table are in the upright position.'

The plane lands with a thud, and screeches. Here we go... into darkness.

I like to refer to Australia as a shit country on the whole, but to be honest it's really beautiful. Unlike me, it's functional.

Everything seems to work really well, from the public transport to the needle exchange system used so that heroin addicts don't spread diseases.

People seem to think Australia is a crime free nation. This is absolute bullshit. Petty crime and gangsterism reign supreme. There are lots of different types of gangs, like the surfer crews who kind of run the beaches. God help you if you drop in to their beach and cut them off while they try to catch a wave, because two things will happen. One, you you'll never be able to go back to that beach and two, you'll get a horrible beating. When I say horrible, I mean it: six, fit, angry surfies wanting to teach you a lesson is going to be a scary experience.

Then you get the Asian gangs. Sing Wa, Lo Sung and Red Dragon. They seem to run the inner city streets. Cross them and you'll probably get stabbed with flick knives and left to bleed out in a dirty ass alley in China town, from what I know about them. Yet they actually care more about money and business than about actual gang banging.

Graf crews like LBM or WFC get mixed up in all sorts of nonsense; there's no hierarchy or order. First of all, there's a dress code, Nike or Addidas, everything. The new Airmax 95's, TN's, LTD's are the usual shoes that you'll see these 'lads' wearing. Nike or Addidas, running shorts and what a surprise, Nike or Addidas shirts. Lastly, they also like to wear Nike visors worn backwards or upside down. Crews usually consist of drug dealers, drug runners, armed robbers, fighters, skaters and the occasional surfie who's converted to the life of crime. They rob young school kids and break into cars (this is called earching). They are known for breaking and entering (B and E's). Even granny bag snatching goes down. All of these crimes are designed for one purpose, quick drug money.

Then if you go out west, you get much more dangerous gangsters: Maoris' and Lebs or Pacific Islanders, people who like to fight and are very good at hurting people.

Then, obviously, you get the big boys, the drug importers, which I believe to be the Chinese or Asian bosses. Also, you get the Russian Mob, which seems to be quite large in Sydney. Lastly, you get the old school pure blooded Australian convicts, who are just brutal, doing bank jobs and the more high class crimes. These types won't hesitate to kill you and throw your body to the sharks.

So tell me Australia is a safe haven…?

In the distance I see my uncle and his crew. They're all looking happy and excited. I must admit that it's very cool to see them; we get along like a house on fire.

My dad cracks a stupid joke, trying to imitate the Australian accent. Everyone seems to think is hilarious, but I don't. We pile into a rented car and follow the other Lancaster's to our first destination.

I should probably say that in all the heartache and pain, there's some excitement. A new place, new people, the ocean and all the goodies that come with immigration are semi-exciting.

Today I know a lot about grief and loss. Obviously at the age of eleven, I knew as much about it as I did about string theory or quantum mechanics. The grieving process is strange; it goes back and forth with bargaining, denial, and anger.

Eventually you reach an acceptance of some kind. I don't think I ever reached acceptance. It seemed to be shadowed by the use of substances, which as you'll see came pretty quickly once I started school.

Chapter 3

This place looks like an old convent; quiet similar to the Cape Dutch style houses in Cape Town except it's cream and the bricks are a lot darker. I fail to understand how they can take these old churches, boarding houses and turn it into a Jewish day school. It looks haunted. Looking around, I'm pretty sure that some fucked up sheep herding bastard will try to touch us when we're alone in the bathrooms. Note to self: Don't go to the bathroom alone.

As I walk through the gates, a new sense of self-consciousness creeps in, like nothing I've ever felt before. The urge to run is massive. I'm so fucking nervous my stomach aches. I know one person in this whole school; it's my cousin who's the same age as me. Everyone around me has this ridiculously thick Australian convict accent. I fucking hate them all already.

Got this gay new uniform on -- khaki pants, coupled with a white shirt, a maroon blazer and the same colour tie. Without the blazer and tie you might confuse me for a young member of the AWB minus the comb in the sock and the gay comb over.

This is high school. I'm still meant to be in standard five, which is still primary school back home. Yet, I've been thrown into high school, not to mention the learning disability I've so freely been given – they call it ADHD. Not really sure what it means, but I do know that I've got the attention span of an egg and I've got to take Ritalin everyday.

I open my mouth to my mother: 'Mom I don't want to be here, please can I start tomorrow?'

'Boy you know you need to start school; there's no time like the present.'

Glorious answer mom, now I'm fully psyched for it, I think to myself.

Why is it that no one thinks of what I want anymore? It always used to be about me and my needs, everything I needed was met, and I had an army of people dedicated to what I wanted. They can't just change it now, can they? It's so confusing.

We head to reception to inform these great people that I've arrived. We walk into a very dull room with a shitty wooden desk that was obviously made by some blind old man with no fingers. There sits an ancient computer and an even older lady behind it. She squints while trying to read some useless information about Bridge or Bowls I suspect.

My mom speaks to the old lady. 'Hi, Nathan is here, can you please inform Ms. Lowe that we're here? She wanted to see Nathan before he started school today.'

My mom then sits down next to me on a horribly worn old school chair, of which the padding is almost bursting out.

'Aren't you a little excited for a fresh start?' she asks with a glimmer of hope in her eyes.

I shatter her hope swiftly: 'You know mom, if I killed someone at my last school and sold guns to small countries and funded civil wars and really needed to leave the country to get into another school, and then I'd have a fresh start, then maybe, just maybe, I would be a little excited…, but I didn't kill anyone and I didn't need to leave the country. So no I'm not excited.'

She looks shocked, she shakes her head in what looks like disappointment, and makes contact with the old bat at the desk.

'Mrs. Lancaster, would you care for a cup of tea or coffee?' she announces her question like a female version of Steve Irwin, the crocodile hunter. Fucking Australians. Sheep shaggers.

'No thanks,' my mom replies, 'I've got to leave now.'

What, did I hear that correctly? You're leaving me here on my own, isolated and with no one near me except the weird whisker lady? Have you lost your mind Mother?

Just as this thought process finishes, she looks at me and says: 'You'll be fine Boy; I'll pick you up at the bus stop at three o' clock. Okay, have a lovely day and good luck.'

Before I'm able to open my mouth she kisses me on the cheek and is out of there faster than I could say no please, you'll be picking me up from the morgue because I'm going to die in here. Three o' clock? That's late. Why so fucking late? These are my lonely thoughts because she is already gone.

I gaze at the floor in paralyzed fear of the old lady. I've got chubby cheeks. I know she's thinking of touching them. I'm going to pretend to sleep. As soon as my eyes close, the infamous Ms. Lowe walks out of her office, with her hand outstretched like she wants to shake my hand. 'Nathan', she says with a big fake smile on her face.

Her short red hair glistens in the morning sunlight that beams through the old stained glass window.

Her pale complexion makes her look Scottish, but you can't hide an accent like that, pure blooded sheep molester.

'Yes madam, I'm Nathan.' I sadly shake the vice-principals hand, it's clammy and wrinkly. It sends shivers down my spine.

'Come with me, I would like to talk to you before we show you around and send you to a class.'

Nathan Daniels

This really sucks, I want to go home.

I follow her down an old hallway filled with pictures of the great achievers of the school. They look like the people I used to bully back home, poor souls. The carpets are unbelievably similar to airplane carpets except they are the same colour as my blazer. We enter a small office with a main desk and two small desks. I wonder why they are there.

'So Nathan, you're twelve right?' She says it still with that smile on her face.

'Yes Madam.'

'Please call me Miss', she interrupts quite rudely.

'You do realise that you're going into high school? We are aware that in South Africa you would still have another year of primary school.'

Get that fucking smile off your face, bitch, before I scream.

'Yes Miss, I do realise this and its okay. I'm sure I can handle it', I say, gritting my teeth.

I need to escape this horrible situation. I'm saved by a knock on the door. 'Come in', she says with absolutely no smile. A young guy opens the door.

'Kevin, I'll be with you in a moment. Please wait outside.'

The door closes hard.

'Nathan, you see these desks', and she points at the two wooden contraptions in front of me.

'Yes Miss,' I reply, trying to act intrigued.

'Well there are these two boys who have been naughty and I gave them in-school suspension; they sit in here all day with me and work so I can watch them.'

She says it with a look that I know too well.

'Let's hope you never land up sitting here mister.'

I shake my head as if that's the last thing that will happen. 'Me? Never, Miss.'

I'm lead into a classroom filled with new strange faces and a teacher with the reddest hair I've ever seen. She kind of looks like she's on fire.

Ms. Lowe introduces me to the class. I feel I'm that fucking loser who comes in all shy and red in the face about to vomit from nerves coupled with low self-esteem. She further embarrasses me by saying 'Don't look down, don't look down, Nathan'.

Three o' clock arrives. The ringing bell signals my freedom that couldn't come soon enough. Today has been a fucking disaster.

I walk nice and slowly to the bus stop. I know my mom is always late, so there's no rush.

I see the bus stop in the distance and some kid fooling around with his friends. It fuels the pain. I miss my friends. I didn't see anyone today who looked like potential friends. I hate this school. I hate the Australians and believe me I'm going to tell my family just how much I hate it here.

I'm the last one at the bus stop. My blood is pumping. How she can do this to me? How can she be late on my first day of school? If that security guard comes and asks if I'm okay, I'll fucking kill myself.

The navy Audi A4 pulls round the corner. I'm going to go ballistic, when she stops here. No, I will just give her the silent treatment that she so hates.

'Hi Boy, so tell me how was your first day?'

I look her in the eyes. 'Not great. Most of the time I couldn't really understand the teachers because their accents are so thick. The kids obviously don't like new students, especially South Africans, because they made fun of me all day.'

'What you mean they made fun of you?'

'Well they were making noises that I suspected was some animal they thought was from Africa and even though they sounded like fucking retards, I knew it was directed at me.'

'Do you want me to speak to the principal?' she says with a seriously concerned look on her face.

'Wow, mom, you really have no idea, I'll be crucified. I'll handle it myself. I'm not a baby, okay?'

'Okay Boy, now what do you want to eat? I can get you McDonalds.'

'Nothing, mom. I really don't want anything to eat. I wish I could tell her what's really on my mind but that would further alarm her.

Fuck food, I'm fat and ugly. The first thing I'm doing here is losing all this weight. I've never been teased. Back home everything was cool. My girlfriend never thought I was too fat. My friends were all basically the same size and I was popular, very popular. So losing weight was never an issue or an option, but things change. This whole fucking plan of immigration is downright stupid. I would give anything to be back home, and I really, really miss my people.

We arrive back home. Dad hasn't started work yet. Cara sits on the couch, looking as miserable as when she had to break up with her boyfriend of four years. I know she really didn't want to lose him. We all had some sort of future back home. Our lives were good. Cara was popular. She had the best looking and most popular guy in school as her boyfriend and a very close knit group of friends that she'd known her whole life. That's exactly what she had: a life.

Fall from Grace

Dad had a super successful dental practice, with a whole team of younger dentists working for him, plus an oral hygienist, plus his own lab in the back. Not to mention all his friends, his golfing days on Saturdays, and a beautiful home that was his own.

Mom probably was most hurt of all of us. She had built up our beautiful home. She basically built up all our lives. She made that huge house a home for all of us, also for all her friends and family. If I'm hurting like this and I'm only 12 years old, I can imagine how she feels after having lived in Jozi for 40 odd years. My poor mother.

I enter the sad little area they call my room. It's half the size of my old room and has a dull single bed with Mickey Mouse covers. Do they think I'm eight years old again?

The cream carpets mark easily. Note to self: Dirty the carpets as much as possible. I sit on the puny matress, which feels like a stretcher. I pull my skates out from under the bed. I can always count on my skates to make me feel better; they always do what I want them to do. I'm in control of them, they can't make their own decisions and that's the way I like it.

I strap them on tightly, and roll around the room a little in hope that I'll mess the carpets, but nothing happens.

'Mom, I'm going down to the beach for a skate, I can't sit in this hole all day.' I say this as an order not a question.

'What Boy? I didn't hear you?'

'I'M GOING TO THE BEACH FOR A SKATE!!!' Frustrated.

'Okay, please be back in time for dinner at seven', she says sounding a little concerned.

'Whatever', I say as I walk out of this pit of negative energy.'

'Whatever mom.'

The air at the beach is beautiful. The salty tang in the air licks my face, and the summer sun shines down on my back. Here is that freedom the old timers spoke of. Its quiet nice, though I'd never tell them that. They must never know I enjoy something here. I skate down the road with an air of confidence. This is the only time I ever feel real. Because this is my identity. I'm a skater, I listen to Nirvana and I skate. Yep that's me.

As I approach the half pipe, I see the usual bunch. This is all really appealing to me: The unbelievable graffiti on the walls, the rubbish in the curbs. I see the kids with long blonde hair and tanned skins. Everything their lives represent is what I want for mine.

'What's up hey?' my role model asks me. 'Not much Dude', I say with that air of confidence dwindling. No eye contact is possible. I'm too shy and too ashamed.

'Where are you from, you got a bad accent?'

I'm from South Africa. I almost called him 'Sir'.

'Fucking hell! That's far away, right?'

I say 'it's far, the plane trip is like fifteen hours and boy was it a fucking horrible flight'. I try my best to start a conversation.

'That sucks Dude'.

He rolls away and drops into the ten foot high half pipe, pulls a huge 360 mute and lands perfectly.

Fuck, yeah, I want to be just like him. To these guys I'm still a beginner. Well I'm only 12, but for my age I can skate. I know these guys know that. Sure as hell they know that.

I take in my surroundings. The beautiful Pacific Ocean stares at me invitingly. Women lie on the beach as if they were at home -- topless.

Crowds of people walk up and down the promenade. Some tourists in the corner are taking pictures of the world famous Bondi beach. On the outside it might be one of the most beautiful beaches in Australia but there lies an underworld, an underworld that draws me in, like a bee to a flower.

As the day falls away so does my and the rest of the guys' energy. They light a fire on the grass next to the ramp. Bottles of beer surround them, and beautiful girls talk quietly among the men. I stare, but I'm too young to get an invite to drink like one of the big guys. That's what I want so badly, to be part of their crowd. I want the blonde hair, the dark skin, the ripped bodies. And of course I want the girls.

With my little fat body, my Jew fro and my unbeachy dress code, I'll never have those things… I'd do anything for it.

Why is life so fucking painful? Why am I filled with this hate and pain? Why is the only joy or peace I experience from drugs or sex or relationships? Why do I constantly search for love in all the wrong places as they say? Why have I been to so many fucking rehabs, so many hospitals, so many psychologists? Why have I taken so many meds? Why do I push away everyone that actually means anything to me? Why can't I live up to my high standards? Why can't I kill myself? Why can't I have faith and understanding? Why does it feel like every moment I'm stepping closer to death? Why do I fuel my pain and heartache by doing the same things over and over? The biggest question of all questions... WHY DID SHE GIVE ME AWAY???

Someone answer me please, why? Why? Why? Please God answer me, tell me why the person who gave me life, the person who was meant to keep me and love me and hold me and make everything right, decided that it was a good idea to give me to a strange family. Why did she do it!?!?!

Where are you? Do you think of me? Do you wonder what I look like? Do you think of me on my birthday? Do you know I've got blue eyes and light brown hair? Do you know that for the last twelve years I've been pumping chemicals into my system to rid myself of anything that resembles a feeling? SOMEONE FUCKING ANSWER ME!!!

Nathan Daniels

You are my mother; you're not supposed to give me away. What the fuck happened mom? I don't even know your name or my dad's name. Do you know I don't want to live anymore? Do you know I cut myself? Do you know that the only time I feel okay is when I have that toxic fucking opiate in my system? Do you know that every relationship I've been in has been a fuck up? Do you know that everything I've tried I've failed at?

Chapter 4

Being down here on Bondi is becoming a daily routine. I'd rather be here than at school. Hey, wait a minute, that's a good fucking idea, Nathan.

Today's a special day: once a year they have this thing called *Big Day Out*.

Today's that day. They've been building this weird ramp and it's massive, maybe 50 feet high. Apparently they're covering it with snow for a big air snowboarding competition. They've been setting up a massive stage, where a few high profile bands are playing. As it can't be Nirvana I don't really care.

I see Tony Hawk, Adam Serlano, and many other pro skaters trying to help set up the mobile skate park. This day's going to be awesome.

'Dom, this is going to fucking rock', I say to my older friend.

'Damn right little guy, you want a beer?'

Wow, he's offering me a beer! I should take it, but I'll smell and get drunk. I desperately want to take it and become one of the boys, but I make an excuse. 'I would Dude, but my rents (parents) are walking on the promenade. They'll come say goodbye and when they go home, I'll have one, is that cool?' I say it as if lying is my strongest asset.

'That's cool Dude, just ask when you want one.'

I'm now part of the beach crew, LBM to be exact, *Lil Bondi Mafia*.

They do graffiti and they do drugs, they listen to hip hop, they drink and have sex with what looks like hot women. These are only the skater beach boys. Then there are those guys that hang around at McDonald's wearing golf shirts, Nike shorts and the best Air Max, not to mention those cool caps pointing backwards. They are thugs. They rob people, fight and deal drugs. These guys are hardcore. I fear them.

Next to the ramp four more possible friends are sitting. They're Julian, Dom's brother Adam, Kevin and Rob.

They all sit and drink beer. I better drink one too.

As I approach them, Dom says: 'You're ready to become a man.'

'I've drunk beer before, it's not like this is the first time Dude', I say acting like I'm sixteen.

'Okay here catch.'

The ice cold Victoria bitter sits in my hand, ready for consumption. I battle with the twist top lid and finally use my shirt to open it.

I take my first sip of the VB and it's exactly what it says – bitter! My nose wrinkles but I can't let the guys see it, so I turn so that my back faces them, acting as if I'm looking at the ocean. I get shivers through my body. Yuk, how am I going to finish this?

I watch as Adam chops up something green in a bowl.

'You ever smoke kronz youngster?'

'No, don't even know what it's, I reply honestly.'

'It's *weed, dope, pot, the green, grass, chronic, hash, Maryjane*. Never heard of it?'

'Oh dope, yeah, I've heard of it, never done it though.'

Fuck, they are doing drugs in such a public place, that's mad. I would love to try it, but I'm scared.

'Today is the best day for it watching the pro's skate. Penny Wise and Silver chair are playing. It's a Saturday and you got nothing to do, you should come to my place later when we go hit the Billy (bong).' He says like a true friend.

'That would be awesome Adam. Let me know when you're going.'

I sit on the grass in front of the boys. I sip my beer and for once in this ridiculous country I feel part of something.

Kevin bumps me and offers me a cigarette. 'Would love one Dude, thanks', I say as I light the cancer stick.

I decide that I'm actually going to take drugs. It scares me a little but not as much as the thought of not having friends, not being part of something. Positive or negative I want it.

Note to self: These guys are my friends. They like me.

The beer tastes horrible. I better drink it as fast as I can to get it over with.

'Dude we're going to my place; you coming or not?' Adam asks me.

'Yeah man I'm coming.'

As the six of us walk up the hill away from the beach I feel strong. I feel powerful. No one will mess with me now, I'm with LBM.

I watch the graffiti they speak of. Chris talks about the piece he did. Amin does the same. I better learn how to do draw like these guys. We approach *Bondi International Backpackers Hostel.*

Is this where he lives? I wonder.

'Now don't make noise in here, I got kicked out of home three days ago and I'm staying here till I find somewhere to stay', Adam says seriously.

That's fucking awesome … so young and he lives alone, doing whatever he wants when ever he wants.

The wall outside the hostel has a massive wave that must tower thirty feet over us.

Chris says it's like Hawaii's surf. We all stand and stare at the massive mural.

'Jesus, wow man, that's mad', are some of the comments flying around.

Adam asks, 'You guys going to stand here all day or we going to get ripped?'

We walk into the hostel like a gang of surfies. In the far corner near an age-old computer and some pamphlets, there's a group of Asian tourists or backpackers standing around looking lost and helpless.

The unkempt receptionist stares in wonder as a small broken fan blows recycled heat around her head, making her hair dance.

I nod at her as we walk past towards the stairs.

Adam's room is a lot bigger than I thought it would be. It's a bedroom with a separate lounge area. Next to this is a kitchen and a small bathroom. The view is unreal.

If I didn't know any better, I'd think this is a nice hotel room.

We all congregate around the coffee table. Adam strolls towards the kitchen and returns with a bowl full with weed.

'Does anyone have mix?' he asks, looking around.

I have no idea what mix is so I just shake my head. Rubin knows what it is, obviously, because he's digging in his pockets saying 'Yeah, I got some.'

He takes out a broken smoke and hands it to Adam, who rips the smoke open and mixes it with the weed. The smell of the green substance floats into my nostrils as he chops it with scissors. A pleasant smell, like nothing I've ever smelled before.

Adam once again leaves the room, and returns with two plastic bottles, a piece of hose pipe and a small silver cone shaped object. Rubin leans over to me and asks 'You ever smoked a bong before?'

'No, I don't even know how it works.'

'Hey guys, Nathan has virgin lungs.'

'Awesome, you have to christen the new bong Nathan', Dom says to me with an evil grin on his face.

'Okay, but I don't know how it works', I say, trying my hardest to act cool.

Adam says 'Its cool Dude, we'll show you.'

The bong is packed and ready for usage. It's handed to me. Adam explains to me how it works. He hands me a lighter and says 'Welcome to the crew lad.'

'Wow I'm part of it for sure now. I blow out, placing my mouth over the top of the bottle. The flame of the lighter dances in the wind. I begin to pull in. The weed ignites. I watch as the bubbles pop in the water releasing the toxin I so desire. 'The bottle if full of smoke', Rubin tells me, 'Now take your finger off the little hole.' As I do that, the smoke which is thick like a piece of cotton wool, shoots past my lips, down my wind passage and into my lungs. My lungs can't handle the stress of all that smoke, so I cough and I cough loudly. The pain is horrible, like when you swallow something and it goes down the wrong way. My eyes begin to water. Barely breathing, I hear giggles, and someone is clapping, Adam taps me on the back as if to say 'Good boy'.

The coughing settles. I look around. The attention is off me. The others pack cones and smoke like this is a natural thing in their lives. It probably is.

'You feel anything Dude?' Dom enquires.

'Not really man.'

'Rubin, pack a Billy for Nathan. He needs to have another one', Dom orders.

Within minutes, the bong is passed to me again. Everyone is focused on themselves getting grilled so no one cares about the virgin lung anymore.

I do exactly what I did last time, except this time I try to hold the smoke in like the others do.

As I exhale, it happens: The room swirls slightly. The sounds are muffled and then heightened. I'm quite scared. Is this it? Is this meant to happen? Should I be feeling like this? I don't know if I like this feeling. It feels out of control. Things are very distorted and confusing. I don't say much. I sit back and wait to see what happens.

I look at Dom. He looks back and asks 'You okay Dude, you white? You feeling it aren't you, little guy?

This might be the funniest thing I've ever heard. I burst out into hysterical laughter, and the more I hear my laugh, the funnier it becomes.

'I don't know, I don't know what is happening here', I say dazed and confused.

'Nathan is now officially stoned people', Dom announces while laughing.

Rubin leans over again 'You're in for the ride of your life, kid.'

I sit back on the comfortable navy couches. I look at the festival going on at the beach, and I wonder if anyone feels as strange as I do?

Ice Cube (the War Disc, to be exact) is playing. Music has never sounded so good. I can single out the beats; I can just hear the bass, then the kick, and then the riff. Ice Cube raps about bitches, hoes, money, thugs, gangsters, drugs, fast cars, and big houses. I like those things, I want those things.

Maybe if I do what Ice Cube does I'll have all those things. I won't rap but I'll thug it out, chill with the boys, take drugs, fight, be a bad ass Motherfucker.

When I think of my friends back in South Africa, I now giggle at the memories of being so fortunate to have had those people in my life. I'll probably miss them forever but right now I've got a crew of brand new friends. I feel part of something, something real, something strong, and something that I'm part of. To go a little deeper, I feel accepted and supported.

At this early part it wasn't about the drugs. I'm not even sure I really loved them. I didn't mind getting high, but I wasn't like this is the best thing ever.

Last night was unreal. In fact I don't know if it was real, it could have been a dream.

The sensation was cool, my reality was distorted. We laughed and had a good time. My senses seemed to be heightened and what I liked was the numbing feeling I got.

I came home and my mom and dad were just sitting down for dinner. I was damn hungry. I sat with them and told them I'd been surfing all day. This was clearly a lie. I couldn't exactly tell them I was chilling in some guy's weird flat smoking weed all day. So naturally I had to lie. I told them my eyes were red from the water and I smelled of smoke because the guys I skate with smoked.

Nathan Daniels

The roast chicken tasted brilliant and I couldn't get enough.

Afterwards I lay on the couch watching the Simpson's and eating a whole bag of milky bars... I then passed out on the couch. I woke up in my bed. What a day.

Australia isn't too bad after all.

I didn't like school; the only things I've ever really liked about school are the girls and the social scene. Studying and all that jazz was never really my strong point. I didn't really have good friends. I was more interested in being friends with the boys at the beach. There were girls though that I liked.

Chapter 5

Finally I got an invite to some stranger's Barmizvah. The only reason this person invited me was because I'm in his class and he invited the whole class. This is a pity invite.

I arrive at the royal yacht club wearing my Shabbat clothes, which these days comprise of a Arctic white SMP collared shirt, a pair of baggy cream cargo pants and my dope DC skate shoes. I feel comfortable in these clothes. I wouldn't dress like Rich boy in his brand new Hugo Boss suit with his Versace tie and Prada shoes. What a fucking show off. I don't like him. He lives in a massive ten million dollar house literally on the harbour with Jet Ski's and a 44 foot ocean master in the exclusive point piper area. Shallow Dickhead.

I don't really know many people here, besides my cousins and a few people from my class. I enter I walk straight up to my cousin Brad and say 'What's up cuzzy?'

'Not much brother, beautiful place to have a barmi hey?' he says, looking real interested in some girl wearing a tight white dress.

'Yeah, it's great', I say, thinking of the sweet sticky weed I smoked about two hours ago.

Just then a thought passes through my head and excites me.

Wealthy family, beautiful place, lots of alcohol and most importantly, good food (not great food). This might not be so bad after all.

'Where is everybody?' I ask, messing around with the buttons on my shirt.

'Downstairs in the ball room', Brad answers with his eyes still fixated on the girl's hind quarter.

I better go say *Mazeltov*. I walk away alone. The only difference is this time I'm stoned.

As I descend the stairs, an old feeling rushes in, that feeling of being insecure.

Suddenly I feel I'm not dressed smartly enough. I now wish I had the Hugo Boss suit and the Prada shoes.

From the crowd lingering around the bar and balcony a hand shoots up and waves in my direction. I can't make out who it is. I turn to look behind me, but there's no one there. So it must be for me. I raise my hand and wave back. The hand then re-appears and waves me over.

I nod and continue my descent. I jump off the remaining stairs. I'm a skater after all. As I land, my ankle buckles under me. This is the most humiliating thing I've ever done: I land hard on the wooden floor and the loud thud emanates around the room. Everyone is silent.

WHAT THE FUCK DO I DO NOW? I do what I know is best. I burst out into hysterical laughter to save myself the embarrassment of someone starting before I do.

A few good doers bend down to help up. A weird old lady with whiskers and yellow teeth asks me if I'm okay.

'I'm perfectly fine', I respond with a blushing smile.

Even though it feels like my knee is out of its fucking socket.

I give it a good rub and a smack to show I'm fine. I proceed towards the bar in search of the attention I so desire.

As I walk past, a few people giggle and ask if I'm okay.

I retort with yeah-yeah, and a very confused look on my face, as if they were talking to the wrong person.

As I approach the bar my sister pops out of nowhere, with that *fucking I know what you did look* and a big fucking grin on her stupid face.

'Are you okay?'

'Yes I'm fine, Cara.'

'Did you hurt yourself?'

'Not really', I respond unenthusiastically.

'Must have been so embarrassing?'

'Fuck off Cara', I say as I walk off.

I wonder who was waving at me. It was a girl… that much I do know.

All of a sudden a hand reaches out and grabs my wrist. It gives me a little fright and a little scream escapes my mouth.

'What's up Girl?' I ask, still looking a bit disheveled from the fall.

'Not much, was it you who fell down the stairs?' she asks, looking genuinely concerned?

'No, poor Fucker in front of me tripped on his laces. It was damn funny though.'

'I know. I heard you laughing', she says while twiddling a finger in her dark brown hair.

'Yeah, couldn't help it really', I laugh. I always laugh from nerves. An awkward silence passes. I bite my lip and say, 'I'm just going outside quickly. I'll be right back.'

'Okay', she says, looking all sheepish.

I turn away feeling quiet pleased with this situation.

For the first time tonight I take in my surroundings, it's actually really beautiful. The perfect white walls compliment the light wooden floor. The bar looks similar to my dad's bar back home in S.A. It looks elegant, not the queens elegant, but the Lancaster's' elegant from South Africa. At that moment I wonder if I could possibly get a drink with a speck of alcohol in it. Maybe later. Let's scope out a spot where I can run off to and take a couple of drags of a smoke.

As I walk outside, the fresh Sydney harbour air caresses my face and hair. The smell from the smokers' corner drifts towards me. It sets off the urge to inhale that nicotine ridden plant.

Usually membership into this club would cost more than money. You could only qualify for this place if you have a massive boat on their water; a Ferrari 599 GTB parked in their garage and of course a enormous house in their area.

Sadly, we no longer have the status or the power to grace this club. Fuck you Rich boy.

The view from the balcony is astonishing, especially at night. I stare at the huge light house in the middle of the beacon.

The semi clear water boasts a wide variety of harbour amenities. I visualized miniature jelly fish coasting the currents, swaying in synchronization with the sea weed. Back and forth, back and forth, back and forth…

The rocks are covered with barnacles lying dormant, corroding in the swell. There's a petrol slick across the water. I know it's caused by million dollar boats that run this precious haven and ruin the small sum of ocean creatures that inhabit the area.

From the view, I can make out the small eroded coast line of Rose Bay. This leads into the hills that make up Vaucluse. I know that the infamous bends on New South Head Road lead to the prestigious all girls' school. The full picture of Beacon isle, sticks out into the harbour. This area consists of the most exclusive areas in the east coast, Vaucluse, Watson's bay, Dover Heights and Diamond Bay.

People hover towards the tables, and the weed is wearing thin. I better eat before it's over. I stroll towards the board designating the table numbers and who sits where. I look for my name. Great, I can't find my name anywhere, just tickle my low self-esteem why don't you. Just fucking great. At least I'm with my cousin Brad.

I fucking hate this stupid shit. As soon as the dinner is over I'm going to find a way of getting a bit of grog in me. I see my cousin keeping me a seat.

'Right here, Cuzzy', he says, waving me over.

'Thanks Boetie', I say, sitting on the seat, which looks more comfortable than my fucking stretcher of a bed.

I peer around to see who else I know at my table.

There's Richard, Nathan and Dean, three dudes from my class who could be friends of mine. They're pretty decent guys. I nod at them and say 'What's up fellas?'

'Not much, hungry Bro', Richard responds, licking his lips.

The other dudes are engaged in a conversation with someone about the swell that's set to hit Bronte and Tamarama in a couple of days.

Note to self: The boys like to surf.

The evening goes along its usual boring ass path. During dinner the MC stands up to announce that speeches will commence in a few minutes.

The people performing the speeches act like it's the most important thing they have ever done. It's downright sad. I need to get out of here now.

I lean towards Richard, 'Dude you wanna go have a smoke?' I ask with a look of desperation.

'Um… yeah, let's go', he leans over to the other fellas and mumbles something.

They all nod.

We all get up and walk to the balcony; there's a little path off the side, which we decide to follow.

We arrive at a small cove, with a few worn down benches.

I pull out my smokes and hand a cancer stick to each of the boys, Mathew has a backpack, he opens it and pulls out a six back of VB. I quiver at the thought of the bitter taste, but I have to drink, plus its alcohol.

We all sit staring out at the harbour view. Not many words are being exchanged, till someone mentions surfing and the conversation gets jump started. They talk about moves I've never heard.

Suddenly I change the conversation to something I can talk about.

'You boys ever smoked weed?' I ask, acting twice my age.

Richard answers 'No, but I like the smell.'

Mathew says 'Nah, but my brother smokes; I could smoke if I wanted, just haven't had the chance.'

Dean says 'Nah, but I remember Mathew's brother toking it up. We could definitely smoke if we wanted. How about you, Nathan? You smoked before?'

'Yeah Dude', I say like a true stoner. 'I smoked earlier today and I've been smoking for a while hey.'

'That's awesome Dude.'

Nods of agreement all round makes me feel like the man.

Richard asks like an admirer, 'Do you think you could organize some for next weekend, I mean we'll give you the money. We could all go to the cliffs and get stoned?'

'Yeah for sure, Dude. I got a cool dealer; he'll pack us fat.'

They nod their heads, not knowing what the fuck I'm talking about.

We finish our beers in basic silence. Occasionally a sentence leaves one of our mouths, but it's mostly quiet.

As we stand to leave, Mathew pulls out some gum and hands each of us a piece. We file into a line and walk back to the party. By now dinner is finished. A few people are dancing. Most people are at the open bar doing what I would be doing, getting drunk.

Then there are all the people of my age. They're sitting outside and talking shit.

I see Samantha and walk over to her. I feel the effects of the beer mixed with the weed. It's not much, but enough to make me feel a little confident.

I walk up and ask, 'What's up Te?'

'Not much, getting tired. Where you been?'

'Um… a couple of us just went to have beer and a smoke.'

'Oh, you smoke? I would love to share a smoke with you.'

'Okay, cool. We can go round to the cove if you'd like to?'

Um… she looks around all nervous, um… Okay, let's go.

'Sweet, I'll be back now.'

I run over to Mathew. 'Dude please let me have another beer and some gum, I'm going round there with Samantha for another smoke?'

'No problem Dude, he says.'

He hands me the backpack – 'Good luck, Dude.'

I walk back over to Samantha and say 'Let's cruise.'

She looks nervous. I wonder what she's thinking.

Should I try to kiss her? No she doesn't like me like that; she just wants to be friends.

We walk round the bend. The clearing is ahead of us. I ask where she wants to sit. There are four benches, she points to the furthest one and says there.

As we walk over, I get mad butterflies.

She sits down and looks up at me. I pull out the smokes; I light one and pass it to her. I pull out another and light it for myself. I then sit down on the eroding bench number two and open the bag. I unleash a beer and look over to her, asking 'Would you like a beer?'

She thinks for a moment and says 'Nah, but I'll have a sip or two if that's okay?'

'Yeah of course, this is my fifth beer anyway'; I don't want to get too drunk, I say, lying like a pro.

Silence falls. It's very uncomfortable. Should I try kiss her? What if she pulls away?

'When did you arrive in Australia?' she asks, also acting really intrigued. 'Um... it was a couple of months ago hey', I say, trying to stare into her eyes.

'So what you think?'

'It's pretty cool.' 'I miss my friends though.'

'Well, you can make new friends here, you know' she says and turns towards me.

'I know, but I don't think it will be the same; my friends there have been my friends since the start.' It's probably the alcohol or the silence but I start to choke up.

'I can be a good friend', she says.

That's definitely a hint; she is staring into my eyes. Her body language says *kiss me*.

I'm going to try. Fuck it, why not? I do like her.

I turn towards her. We fall silent again…Samantha did become my girlfriend, my first Aussie girl.

Chapter 6

The stupid fucking bus ride is taking its time. Adam should be waiting for me. I take out the money that sits in my tight pocket and begin counting it for the sixth time. 20, 40 all the way up to 120… You see it costs hundred dollars for the quarter ounce of weed I'm getting for some older Dudes at school. I should be paid for my services though. I see Adam outside MacDonald's and I leap to the front of the bus.

'Driver, please can you open the door, I can see my bus to school and I can't miss it.'

'Okay, young man, you better run or you'll miss it.'

The doors open, I descend the stairs and jump onto the pavement. I cross the road in front of the driver. He hoots at my defiance. I stick up my middle finger and run off towards McDonald's.

I want to get high.

I greet my good friend with a Bondi slap.

'What's up Bro?' says Adam.

'Not much at all Dude, just wanna smoke before school, you in?'

'Yeah Dude, I took the liberty of chopping some of the chronic and rolling a spliff so you can test it before you slang it.'

'Good stuff, where do you wanna smoke?'

'Let's go into that alley in between the bus depot and the train station … we can smoke and do the deal.'

'Sweet'. We both head in the direction of the alley. The excitement builds. I love smoking this early in the morning.

Adam hands me the joint he rolled prior to meeting me. It's not really a joint, it's more like a fucking baseball bat, it's huge.

We enter the alley; it's really run down and fucked up. I feel comfortable here. Adam never seems comfortable. His eyes shift all over, looking for the DEA agents he suspects are following his every move.

'Here, quick Bro, take the shit.'

He sticks his hand into his waist line and pulls out the bud. It's an ounce bag filled up quarter way. It really looks good.

We exchange the product and the cash. I put the bag in my pocket. 'What the fuck are you doing? Ball that shit Dude, you can't walk around with that in your pocket.'

'Whatever way … you paranoid fuck'; I say while shoving the weed into my groinal area, '…it looks weird Dude.'

'Spark that shit, I need to go. Fuck it Bro, let me spark it.' He takes the spliff and lights it. It's so big. I laugh when he lights it.

There's an unwritten rule about smoking a spliff with someone. More like a process actually. It goes puff, puff, pass. Adam breaks this rule every time and then shouts 'If you don't stick to the rule, today is different.' Adam's paranoia is rubbing off on me; I just want him to go. He passes me the blunt.

'I'm going Bro, meeting the fellas for a surf', Adam says looking in the sky for the DEA scum in helicopters.

'Sweet Bro, I'll catch you later'. A Bondi shake and he's off into the distance.

I'm left with this massive joint, enough weed in my pants to send me to juvenile for the rest of my life. Better smoke this quickly and get the fuck out of here.

As I token the spliff, smoke engulfs my area.

The bus ride to school is a lot better than the bus ride to the junction, because this time I'm stupidly stoned. My eyes are almost closed due to dryness. I rub them and this makes them worse.

As I walk through the gates of this hell hole, the urge to run is overpowering. Fuck school, let me do this deal and scram to the beach. Still got forty minutes till retarded prayers. Enough time to smoke a bong or two.

I make my way down to the bathrooms in the music department, where all the bad asses smoke.

The last cubical in the change rooms is meant for disabled folks, it's a fucking huge cubical, almost the same size as my pathetic room.

I stand on the bench; lift up the trap door in the roof, to remove my bong. I grab my bag; remove my diary with my name sprawled across it, and my pair of scissors. I tax a bit of the bud from the ounce bag. I chop the bud, the sweet smell of the THC floats into my nostrils. I fucking love it!!!

I prepare the cone piece, just as I steady the bong near my mouth. I hear the main door to the change room open. I freeze, lift my feet onto the toilet, and stop breathing.

'Mr. Lancaster we know what you're doing in there', a voice bellows out.

I choke up, my head spins, and I might faint or vomit.

'Now Mr. Lancaster come out of there.'

What the fuck? I'm dead. I can't believe I'm about to get expelled.

Suddenly I hear two people burst out laughing. I recognize Pat and Ari from their stupid ass stoner laughter.

'Very fucking funny, Cocksuckers. I almost had a heart attack.'

'Open up Bro, let us have a bong', Ari murmurs while still laughing.

'Whatever', I say, opening the door.

After two bongs the door opens again. This time it's serious.

'Nathan, you in there? It's Dan; Ms. Hottie is looking for you. I thought I would come get you before she finds you.'

'Thanks Dude.'

'Boys, just leave the shit here. I'll be back to pack it away.'

'Sweet… Dude, good luck. I hope she licks your balls', Pat says while laughing.

'Fuck it me too Bro, she's hot', I say leaving the cubical.

I walk up the stairs wondering what's going on, why would the *hotness* want to see me?

I see her in the distance. I walk towards her.

'Oh Nathan I've been looking for you, where you been? 'the Sperb asks me.

I've been in the bathroom, my stomach really hurts.

'You should go see the nurse. Anyway your mum called me this morning; she won't be able to pick you up today, so you can get the bus. Do you have money on you?'

'Yes I do, thanks for the message Miss.'

'No problem', she says and walks away. I stare at her cute ass as she walks away. Beautiful sight, I must say.

I descend the stairs to the bathroom. The minute I touch the door handle, the last fucking voice I want to hear calls out: 'Nathan where are you going? Ms Lowe cries with that nasty ass streak in her voice.

TO THE FUCKING BATHROOM TO SMOKE A FAT CONE, WHAT THE FUCK IS IT YOU WANT FROM ME? Just thoughts.

'Nowhere Miss … to the bathroom.'

'Not now. You will help set up in the hall, for once!'

'But Miss… my stomach…'

'Bullshit, your stomach nothing, you will follow me up the stairs right now.'

OH MY GOD, I HOPE YOU FALL WHILE WE WALKING UP AND YOU SMASH YOUR FUCKING TEETH OUT, YOU HORRIBLE HUMAN BEING.

'Now come, she starts walking up the stairs.'

I follow her fat ass up the stairs. It's okay … Straight after prayers; I'll run back and pack everything away.

Prayer time is fucking long. Thank God I'm semi-stoned otherwise I would die.

Prayers end and I run down the stairs, I open the door, and dash straight into the change room.

The cubical door was left open, fucking idiots.

I walk in and my greatest fear was come true: Everything is gone. Maybe the Fuckers took my bag, and put the bong back. I jump on the bench and look in the roof. It's not there. Maybe they put it somewhere else to scare me again.

I search everywhere, every cubical, every stall. Nothing.

The bell rings to signify math's class. I can't do anything about it now. I'll deal with this after class.

I sit in this boring ass math's class. My stomach churns my heart races.

There's a knock on the door and Ms Lowe walks in. She says something revolting in hushed tones to the math's teacher.

'Nathan please can I have a word?' Ms Lowe utters.

My heart sinks. Fuck it, I'm busted. It's been a good run. Fucking bitch.

We stand outside the classroom.

'Listen, Nathan, I need you to be honest with me. We found your bag in the bathroom downstairs.

'Oh is this what it's about, yeah … I left it here yesterday.'

'Well it has a big bag full of Cannabis in it. Also we found something serious lying next to it. Are you aware of what I'm talking about?'

'No Miss, as far as I'm concerned, I don't have any Cannabis in my bag, nothing serious either.'

She stares into my eyes, to see a flinch, something to give her an idea that I'm lying. But nothing comes. I've perfected my lying technique.

'Okay, well go back into class, and come get your bag after this.'

'Will do Miss', I say, turning my back heading towards the class room door.

The rest of class goes on like normal, boring and tedious.

I make my way up to witch's office, to get my bag. She has no proof the

weed is mine, so I'll deny it till I'm blue in the face.

I knock on her door. As I open the door I see my parents inside. My stomach wrenches, my heart drops, and I might throw up. I know what's coming.

Not to self: I'm DONE!!!

The drive home is something I've got to get used to. Dad gives his usual

lecture and mom sits in a disappointed huff.

'Nathan, what were you thinking doing all that shit at school? If you want to smoke those twigs with your friends, then you will deal with the consequences but when you take that shit with you to school and smoke it, then this becomes a family issue, I mean, do you have any idea how embarrassing this is for us all? You make the family look bad! What you got to say for yourself?'

I stay silent. 'Well what you got to say?'

'Nothing I'm, nothing.'

'Nathan', my mom says, 'you better answer me, why are you doing this? What did you do this for?'

I think of why I did this, and no answer comes to mind. I honestly don't know why. 'I don't know Mom, I don't know why I did this.'

'Well, that's not good enough. I want a proper answer Nathan', my mom says horribly.

'I don't fucking know Mom.'

'DON'T YOU DARE USE THAT LANGUAGE TO YOUR MOTHER, DO YOU HEAR ME?' My dad says furiously.

Silence falls in my dad's gay RAV 4 Max.

It's weird being able to look back on the times when I was clearly out of control, when the consequences were starting to get really hectic. Yet I really couldn't see the problem. I just outwardly blamed my family, or the immigration. Denial is a strange thing; it allows me to blame everything but myself. It allows me to keep on using. Before it got bad it made a lot of sense.

Chapter 7

The drive to St Josephs College Boarding School is very long and extremely boring. My dad listens to golden oldies, my mom's very quiet. You should all know that this is my father's fault anyway. Plus I know my parents will fold when we get there. I've heard these threats since I was a young bean. 'Nathan, if you do this again, you're going to boarding school.' It's never really happened though, so ultimately this is just a road trip to some prestigious Catholic boarding school. Also, I'm Jewish. I can't go pray to Jesus now.

This is a bit more serious than anything I've ever done before but it's my dad's fault, so I don't care. None of this would've happened if we were still in South Africa, so fuck him.

'Nathan, this school is very good. It's the top rugby school in Sydney and it's full of high achievers.' My dad says this sounding like he just read the brochure that sits on my lap.

It actually looks really big and beautiful on paper but there's such a thing as trick photography. I begin to wonder … What if they are serious this time. What if they leave me here? No, no they wouldn't do that to me, would they? I guess this pushed them or him quite far. But my mom always has my back, she wouldn't let this happen.

I belong at home in our big house in Vaucluse with my view of the harbor and my secret hidden bong in my old school blazer.

Fall from Grace

What if they do leave me here? What am I going to do about my new life? Where am I going to find weed out here at this school of Jesus?

We drive up to the main gates of the school. I'm suddenly overwhelmed by the sheer size of the gate. It looks like a holy monster awaiting its victims. The victim in this case is an innocent Jewish kid who is obviously misunderstood, and very unhappy because his father decided to ruin his life. Can't anyone see that this is not my fault?

We are greeted by Mr. Rolls Royce, Mr. Bentley and many other exclusive cars that cost more than our house. Awesome, I don't feel inadequate driving up in this brand new Audi, which in this situation was like a go cart.

We stop behind a Bentley. The famous flying spur, laughs at me as I get out of the go cart.

I watch as the owner of the Bentley (a rather large man), hands his son (a rather larger boy), enough Australian cash to support my habit for months. Lucky fuck.

I admire the old building towering over us. It's an old building and has probably been around since the time of Jesus.

I don't like it here. I'll probably be blamed for the death of Jesus by the students and teachers alike. Fuck this. I want to go home.

'Come Boy', my dad says so hopeful, 'we must go find the supervisor of your standard.'

My mom is still silent. Come on Mom, back me up.

I grunt, look at my mom's swollen eyes, and head up to the second floor of this gargantuan building.

The first floor is teaming with students, brothers and of course the very well-off parents.

Nathan Daniels

This place smells like blood, sweat and tears. I don't want to think about the food here. This number of students means big vats of cheap food. Yuk... I'm suddenly feeling sick.

We make our way up the stairs to the second floor. The stairs are worn down and this makes the edges round and slippery. There are pictures on the walls of archbishops, brothers, fathers, and of course priests, a few nuns. There are also paintings that look like they belong in a gallery somewhere.

Suddenly an enormous man greets my father.

'Mr. Miller', my dad says with his hand outstretched.

'Yes, who might you be?' he asks, looking very interested.

'I'm Dr Lancaster, this is my wife Fiona, and here is my son Nathan.'

'Pleased to meet you Dr, Mrs., Nathan.'

'I believe you've spoken to Brother Jeff, he has instructed me to show you folks around this historical place.'

Historical? Please don't insult me, there was no such thing as history when this thing was built, I think to myself (because no-one here would appreciate my joke).

'Um... I'll show you folks the dorms first. Now these dorms were used during World War 2 as hospital wards. They were converted to dorms when this building became a monastery in the late seventies.'

What the fuck? Hospital? Monastery? Dead people, the father the son and the Holy Spirit? Mom, you can't leave me here; it's haunted with holy ghosts and dead angry soldiers.

TAKE ME HOME PLEASE, I'LL STOP SMOKING. PLEASE, I DON'T WANT TO BE POSSESSED BY AN ANGRY SOLDIER OR A HOLY PERSON. These thoughts are just thoughts. I've learned as a

Fall from Grace

child never to interrupt someone speaking. So this panic falls away. 'This is the main dorm', he says, showing us an appalling sight.

A hundred beds stacked right next to each other. There's a very small locker where I reckon, they expect you to keep one shirt, one pair of pants and the nasty school uniform they want us to wear.

Just then I see a familiar face, Dom Con…

Dom spots me and waves me over. I tell the Fuckers that I'm going to say hi to Dom.

As I walk past all the beds I notice that everyone has computers and phones and all sorts of goodies I don't have. There's a fat kid sitting on the bed next to Dom's bed.

'What's up Bro?' Dom says, putting out his hand.

I slap his hand in the way we slap from our area, just to make sure we do know each other.

Our hands are synchronized, we know what's up.

'Not much Bro, just taking a look around', I say, looking arrogant and hardcore.

'Why, what happened to Emmanuel?'

I look around to make sure no-one else is listening. Then I say, 'I got expelled for smoking and dealing weed.'

'Serious?' 'Yep, you're staying Dude. This school takes expelled kids and tries to reform them. Like myself and a few others, it's not actually that bad here Bro. This is my second term, the first was awesome, we smoked loads of bud, hooked up with fluff from St Mary's and just had some real fun down at the river and shit. Where's your stuff? You can bunk next to me?'

Just then Harrison, the fat American kid, whom I first saw, looks up and says 'but I bunk next to you!'

'Shut up tubby, you're going to move or trust me I'll make you move!'

Harrison quickly shuts his mouth and gets up to leave. 'Go say something to the prefect's fatty and I swear you'll live to regret it', Dom says with a very serious look in his eyes.

'Remember Harrison, you can't get away from me, you do sleep fat boy.'

Wow, that was heavy.

Note to self: I don't let Dom know, but I'm fat as well, so I take a little bit offence. Never mind though.

'I didn't bring anything with me, I'm just looking around'. I say, looking towards the enormous man followed by my parents. 'I better go, they're waiting for me.' Once again, we do our familiar handshake. 'Take care Bro', I say as I turn around and head back to those traitor parents of mine.

'Shall we continue our tour?' asks the oversized man, Mr. Miller.

The rest of the boring tour I do alone. Apparently my parents have gone to speak to the head master.

'So Nathan, you excited about becoming a Joey?'

'A Joey? A baby kangaroo? What the fuck are you talking about man?'

'Yes, a Joey. That's what we call people who enroll in this school!' Mr. Miller says this with a smirk that only a *Joey* could pull off.

'Yes I am', I say, lying once again, 'but I need to go home discuss this with my parents and pack some stuff for my stay.'

'No need Young lad, your parents will be back this weekend to visit and they took the liberty of packing a small bag with everything you need for right now.'

WHAT? This time I can't hold in the feelings of betrayal, they've left me here? I run to the window to see if the silly car still sits behind the Bentley. It's gone. THESE FUCKERS LEFT ME IN A HAUNTED BUILDING FILLED WITH ANTI-SEMITES AND THE WORST OF ALL NO WEED OR MONEY TO BUY WEED. WHAT THE FUCK AM I GOING TO DO NOW? 'Where is my stuff?' I ask, not expecting the answer I get.

'Let's get a few things straight before we go on', Mr. Miller's eyes suddenly turns malicious.

'You will address me as sir, lord or God, I'm not fair or reasonable, people often call me a prick. I hate kids, especially fat little shits with no respect for themselves or anyone around them. You're a budding drug addict and trust me I'll get you right if it's the last thing I do.'

He pulls me closer to him; I can smell his disgusting breath. 'Plus you step out of line here and there's no going home. I will come in here while you sleep and give you the beating of your life, you hear me Scum bag?'

'Yes', I say, shivering a little.

'Yes what?' he shouts out.

'Yes prick', I say' fearing the worst.

He laughs a fucking evil hackle, good start. I'm going to be all over like green on grass punk.

Just as fast as it started, it ended. I'm left standing alone, hurting. This pain is very different. Rejection from the people who were meant to love me and protect me.

Now they leave me with the modern day version of a Freddy Kruger.

TRUST ME I'LL REMEMBER THIS FUCKERS, I'LL REMEMBER.

I need to cry. Can't do it here. Hold it in.

within moments Dom is behind me. 'Don't worry Bro all the bad boys here get that treatment from that Cocksucker and the parents leaving you behind. Miller suggests it to all our parents. Welcome you're one of us.'

Joyous. I don't really know him or what I'm getting myself into, but I'd rather be part of whatever he speaks of than be alone in here.

'Come on Bro, let's get your stuff and unpack it into your space.' Harrison, fuck off and go find another bed. I'm serious Dude. FUCK OFF.'

Harrison sits in silence acting like he never heard Dom. Dom slaps Harrison quite hard. Well, hard enough to jar the little ball of fun into an immediate action of packing. Within moments, Harrison is gone. I unpack into the small locker. I feel dizzy. Dom reassures me that all the guys around us have been through what I just went through. He then introduces me to the boys who surround us. Across me is Julian, not sure what race he is. I think he is Indian, but I'm not sure, He could be from one of the Islands that surrounds Australia, I don't know. Then there's Blake. Blake was a fellow pot head. He was expelled from a few schools for the same offense I was. Apparently Blake has a hot mom; well that's what Julian says. Then of course there's Marcel. Now Marcel is a special case, people believe he is actually mentally disturbed. Apparently Marcel's dad is one of the richest men in the world; he owns an Island that they go to on holiday, a fleet of super cars that tower above anyone else's in this school. He also owns the rights to Panado for the whole Island of Australia, which I guess is big deal.

We all lie in our beds till lights out… We are talking and telling jokes. The lights go out suddenly. 'Good night Fuckers', someone yells out (Marcel I suspect). 'What's the time?' I ask Dom? 'Dude, it's nine o'clock.'

This can't be real or can it?

Chapter 8

This cold winter morning starts off as fucking usual. Some Dickhead prefect walks through our dorm with a cow bell attached to his hand. He is ringing and dinging till everyone who sleeps in this dirty place are on their feet. As soon as the tosser leaves, everyone (except the ass lickers) jump back into their warm beds. Winter is brutal out in this part of the country and the prefects like to open the windows when we all sleep (not in our corner though).

The prefects learnt a hard lesson, the morning after Nathan B arrived. One of the brave elders came into our corner and tried to stretch over Nathan to get to the window. Little do they know Nathan was to be the youngest golden glove boxing champ of this decade. As Marcus leaned across he got a vicious uppercut, shattering three of his teeth and almost cutting his tongue right off. He screamed out in pain, blood spilling all over the worn carpet. To my shock, the prefect tried to contain Nathan once again, but like an animal backed into a corner, Nathan lashed out and caught the prefect on the corner of his chin. Silence fell among the crowd as the prefect's eyes rolled back and he tilted like a doll. His head hit the floor with a thud and that's where it stayed. He was carted out of our dorm by three other prefects. That was the last of our window being opened by the Dickheads.

'What's up Bro, fuck its cold this morning', I say, still struggling to open my eyes.

Nathan Daniels

'I know it sucks, let's get warm and go blaze up before breakfast what you reckon?'

'Sounds good Bro', I say as I stand to get on three layers of school uniform.

Dom leans out of bed and calls Julian who sleeps opposite me.

Nathan pipes up, 'Nathan you plank, why you putting on school clothes, it's Saturday?'

Feeling like an idiot, I shrug and laugh it off. Within minutes I'm dressed and listening to Dom who tells Julian he will organize him a hundred dollar phone card for two sticks. (A stick is twenty dollars worth of weed or one gram).

Julian reluctantly agrees. He knows he can pawn the card off to the Asian rich kids for at least fifty bucks so he takes the bait and hands over the bud.

Dom gives me one to keep and pockets the other. 'Let's go Dude', he says.

We walk off, past the prefects lounge and down the stairs. The walk to where we smoke is cold and wet. I rattle on about how much I hate it here. Dom agrees: 'It is a horrible place to be'. Secretly, Dom is my hero. He has hooked up with the girls I always dreamed of, he deals drugs and he has done ecstasy, cocaine and many other drugs that I've never heard of. I want to be more like him, so every morning we go get high. I sit and listen in as he tells me about his adventures in and around Bondi.

When we get to our secret spot behind the storage facility, an older guy sits smoking our bong in our spot. Dom seems to know him, and asks 'What's up?' He finishes his last cone and quickly walks off towards his dorm.

Dom hands me the scissors and the piece of paper, in the paper sits a bud that would allow three or four bongs each. I take out the smokes in my pocket and break one in half. I love this ritual … the weed's aroma float about my nostrils. Once I'm done, the golden rule I so love falls into place: The person who chopped gets the first cone. I drop the cone with zealous

Fall from Grace

greed. The effects of the THC aren't what they used to be. It makes me feel normal rather than high.

We line up in the dining room awaiting our food of dry toast and oats.

Mr. Miller sits at the head of our table. Our crew sits right at the other end as far away from that prick as possible.

The oats with milk and lots of sugar satisfies the munchies for about an hour. Then it's off to the garage to buy some real food.

Saturdays are really decent here; we're allowed to go down to the river to watch the rowing, which means we can run around the area for like four hours with no problems. We often go get more weed for the rest of the week, we also get munchies, or we go see the girls across the river. There's a spot under the bridge where loads of girls and boys gather to forget their sad lives of being abandoned and left to die in boarding school. Drugs are taken, alcohol is drunk and once or twice we're all forced to run away from a nun or a brother.

'Why we not leaving the school? 'I ask Dom.

Cos you see my friend, it's the big race today. Most of the school go and cheer on our "Joey's". They are facing the biggest rivals we have Kings College.

Everyone who stays behind are either too old to walk all the way down to the river or they are sick. Therefore the school becomes ours, we can smoke as much as we want, or do whatever we like. He's so cunning; I need to learn this stuff.

By two o'clock Julian and Dom are sleeping. I'm bored, so I go have a ciggie in our secret spot.

As I'm about to drop the smoke, I double clutch: A voice I shudder to hear, emanates around me. 'You're so fucked', Mr. Miller points out from the roof above my head. Once again I'm caught red handed, fucked, done, and scared that the beating he always threatens is on its way.

He jumps down and lands right in front of me.

'So Sunshine, what you going to say now?' he says, standing over me.

'Got nothing to say Sir.'

'So, I'm not a prick anymore?'

'No Sir. Please can we work something out? I can't get into trouble again.'

'What do you suggest? he says.'

'No idea, I promise this won't happen again though Sir.'

'Too late for that. You're already in trouble.'

'Go to my office and get ready for the lashing of your life.'

I walk away from the crime scene, feeling frightened of what lies ahead.

I think of the cuts and open wounds, Julian showed us after he got caught

smoking. It sends a shiver down my spine.

There's a way out though, not sure of the consequence but it would be better than getting smashed with that bamboo whip. I knock on the Headmasters door.

'Come in', Brother Jeff says with compassion and love.

'Oh… Nathan', how are you. Young man?

'Not great Brother', I say, looking nervously at the lasses of my shoes. 'Is something the matter?'

Fall from Grace

'Yes Brother, Mr. Miller just caught me smoking a cigarette.' A disappointed look falls over his face, 'Take a seat young man.'

Brother Jeff presses a button on his phone and tells Sister Margaret to bring in my file. He looks through a few pages then says, 'My son, I'm going to have to suspend you till next weekend. I'm going to phone your parents to come pick you up right away. You need not return if you don't want to obey the rules of this school. Do you understand me?'

'Yes Brother'. I say as innocently as I can.

'Now go pack your stuff and wait till your parents arrive. If you do want to return to our school then come back with the right attitude, think about your life and which direction you want it to go. I expect a 2000 word essay on your honest opinion to where your life is going. Now go and behave for this week. Please give your parents a break! Back in the dorm, I wake Dom.

'Dude wake up, I got caught smoking...'

'Smoking what Bro?' he asks really concerned all of a sudden.

'Winfield Blue, luckily.'

'So what's happening then?' he asks, now sitting up.

Note to self: Brother Jeff is suspending me for a week, which is actually quiet cool, my own bed and house for a week, to tell you the truth I'm not bothered by it.

'Your rents are going to flip out though?'

'They'll get over it', I say while packing.

'Don't worry Bro; we'll have a good time.' He says with that smile that I've grown to know.

'It takes a second to register, what do you mean we?'

'I'll be home tomorrow night Bro', he says.

'What, how, why?' I ask, looking rather confused.

'Fuck it, why not; we can get a hotel, some coke even some pro's if you want? Okay man just don't be silly, don't get kicked out.'

'Don't worry Bro, I know this school back to front', he says as I begin to walk away.

'See you Tomorrow Bro', he says while smiling the smile.

I'm greeted by the fucking shadow of Mr. Miller as I walk into the empty hallway, I'm clipped on my ear hard, and it hits the inner bell inside my head because all I can hear is a ringing.

'You think you're so fucking smart, Jew boy, going to the brother to sort out your problems.'

'Well, if you think you've escaped me, you've just dug your hole a lot deeper. Boy, please step into my office for a quick chat before you have a great week with Mommy and Daddy.'

I find myself bent over his table with my pants around my ankles. He circles like an angry shark with the whip in his hand. Cursing my Jew God and blaming me for the death of Jesus, just then it happens… WHACK, WHACK, WHACK!!! The pain isn't that bad, maybe I go into shock or he hits so hard that it goes numb first. After the ninth whack I'm in agony, he must have gone over the same cut three times. I pull back from the table. I stumble and fall on my bum, and as I stand, I see the blood stain on the floor. I gently touch my fat Jewish ass as he put it, and see the blood running down the back of my legs.

He drops the whip and tells me to go to the nurse. As I leave, he says, 'Try fuck with me again and this will seem like a fucking massage.'

I begin to cry as I walk down the remaining stairs. I wait for my parents in the cold, trying to sit on the area of my bum that wasn't thrashed by that maniac. *Don't worries* I keep telling myself, he'll get his, what goes around comes around.

Funny enough, he did get his in the week I was away. He grabbed Nathan in the shower for pissing on some small kid. Apparently Nathan climbed into the tall man, breaking a lot of his ribs, his nose and his jaw. Also, the most harsh consequence was that he hit him so hard under the eye, that Miller lost some of the sight in his left eye… Serves you right, bitch.

Nathan now sits in juvie. He got charged for assault with a deadly weapon. Miller took a much less risky job in the school. He is now head of the kitchen.

Chapter 9

The suspension was a fucking holiday: My queen size bed, satellite TV, as much food as my hungry stoned stomach desires and as much weed as my heart desired.

Meanwhile, back at the ranch, school was going back to its usual slow bull shit. The bell in the morning, the cold, the breakfast bongs, the lack of females, not to forget the sick, twisted way of this cesspool of pedophiles. Fucking brothers, sisters and fathers, it's all a bit of incest for me, plus that anti-Semitic class we had: I think they called it 'religious studies'. I'm surprised they didn't start a fucking witch hunt for the only Jew in the school. You know, tie me up, burn me at the stake, for killing their make believe Son of God… Whatever, I think people can believe what they want. My argument is if someone is a man of God, then why the fuck doesn't that God, bless that person.

Why do so many kids fall victim to the abuse of some old wrinkly balled "fathers"? It makes me feel sick. I swear, if some Motherfucker had to try make a pass at me or touch me, I'd let out generations of anger, torture the poor Fucker till pain or exhaustion stopped me. Nevertheless, he would suffer a great deal of pain.

'Morning Nathan, great to have you back with us', Miller says with the smile of victory on his fucking face.

I continue walking, without greeting or lifting my now tilted head, straight passed that evil man who looks like he just went a couple of rounds with Iron Mike. He is now in charge of the food we eat, I don't know which is

Fall from Grace

worse, him with that whip or him with a recipe book. Either way, I'm glad that Karma got involved in my situation…

Note to self: Thanks Karma for intervening.

On my return to this hell pit wrapped in a nice shiny cover, the head pedo told me that I'm standing on my last leg. Should I break one rule, even the slightest, smallest rule, I will be out. So I've been trying harder not to get caught doing the bad shit I do.

It's the last day of the term, it's exams. For once in my life I was forced to study. I still don't really know my work. Most of the time I was going through shit loads of paper practicing my new found talent (graffiti). But I guess it looked like I was writing, so I was never really bothered.

As usual, the need to get high arises at dawn just like the sun. I make my way to my own secret hiding spot that no one knows about (not even my friends know where I go to get high). I figured this was the safest way to get away with it and so far it was working.

I sit on my makeshift seat, a rotting log that has actually formed a small worn part where my scarred bum sits every day. I pull out the bong from the inside of yet another hollow log. It's filled with insects, that would've died from either drowning or getting stoned from the toxic hydro infested water. The weed is packed, the sweet sweet *Mary Jane*, burns its beautiful toxins out into my lungs… Right on schedule, the THC fumes absorb into my blood stream, and within seconds I can feel the effects. I repeat the process a few times, satisfied that I'm finally high enough to box with God. I pack away all my goodies and head off to my English exam.

Time ticks and I'm late. I can't find my school bag, which means no pen to write the god forsaken exam. There are five minutes till it begins. I go into a manic panic. My locker might have a pen. The hall where my locker stands is empty. If I can't find a pen in my locker, I'll take one from someone else's. The locks on these lockers are stupid, if you pull the door hard enough it opens. Mine stays open all the time; I got nothing worth stealing anyway. Nothing is in my locker, who would steal my text books? Fucking weird.

Nathan Daniels

I pull the locker next to mine, nothing inside. Then the next and the next. I see a pencil case with the name Tyrone on it. Fuck it, I'm taking it.

I open the pencil case and look around, I take out a pen and look around, two minutes till the exam. I look around, put it in my pocket, and as I look around for the third time, I stare into the eyes of Miller, the cock sucking abusive pervert, who has clearly caught me in the act of stealing this pen. Surely he won't tell anyone, it's just a pen for fuck sake.

'I've been waiting for this day; I've been watching you, waiting for you to slip up. I know what you've been up to. I just had no proof, but now I do, you're done Jew boy, you're done.'

'Fuck you Miller, you sick sadistic fuck, you been watching me in the shower as well haven't you?' I say with rage building.

He strides towards me, covering an amazing amount of area with each step. I look for a weapon. There's nothing around, should I run? No, point is he has caught me, what about my exam?

He grabs my arm with a vise like grip that I'm now used to.

'Get your grubby hands off me, you Sick Fuck', he slaps me over the head, not that hard, but a slap nonetheless.

'You're coming with me to see Brother Jeff right now', he says with the glint of mania in his eyes.

'If I go down, you coming down with me Miller', I say, thinking of the lies I can make up.

'I haven't done anything wrong for you to pull me down', he says, eyes shuffling.

'Really, you might know that, I know that but it's my word against yours. I will make up so many stories they will echo for years in court and at this shithole of a God loving school, you know what? Fuck you, I'm a Jew and

I'm fucking proud of it, you just jealous because we're the chosen ones. Try me and watch me crucify you just like my people did, those many years ago.'

He stares in wonder for a few seconds, 'I don't care what you do, first I'm going to beat you black and blue, and then I'm going to say that you attacked me and I hit you in self-defense'.

'Whatever Fuck-head, a man of your size hitting me in self defense when you could have subdued me, I'll sue the fuck out of this school and by the end of the year, you'll be homeless.' I now say, thinking of ways to kill this tyrant.

We arrive at Brother Jeff's office, the last few steps, we think of our stories.

Miller knocks firmly on the old oak door.

'Come in', Brother Jeff says with that air of compassion.

Miller pushes me in first.

'Nathan? What's going on?' Those disappointed eyes focus on me again, then on the beast, and then on me again.

Miller pipes up before I can say anything, 'I caught him stealing, brother'.

'Is this true Nathan?' The disappointment deepens.

'Not really brother, I was borrowing a pen for my exam', I couldn't find my bag so I had no pen to write English, Sir'. I say this pulling out my puppy eyes.

'Whose pen did you take?'

'Tyrone's pen Sir', I say, still trying to look innocent.

Nathan Daniels

'Does Tyrone know you were taking his pen?' Jeff asks, looking abit more hopeful.

'Um… no brother, but I wasn't going to keep it, I'm sure Tyrone wouldn't have minded if I borrowed his pen, he's in my class after all.'

'Nathan that's called stealing, no matter which way you look at it', brother

says looking out the window now.

I fall silent, Miller smirks.

'Mr. Miller you may leave, I'll take it from here', Brother Jeff says nodding him towards the door. 'Thank you brother', he says, while walking towards the door.

Fucking Dickhead, I'll ruin him before I leave this portal to hell.

'Nathan, I'm sorry to have to say this, but I laid down the rules to you when you came back. You stole, and that's breaking a big rule. I'm not suspending you again.

Thank God, I'm staying. One of the thoughts running around my mad head.

'Please sit down young man', he offers the chair.

I take the chair. The weed has worn off, I'm in trouble, but at least I'm staying here.

Like *déjà vu*, he picks up the phone, sister please bring me Nathan Lancaster's file.

What is going on? I think it's just going on my record or something. Maybe he wants to tell my rents what a bad boy I am.

I sit quietly awaiting my fate.

Fall from Grace

He picks up the phone once again and dials my dad's number.

'Hello Jeff', he says still looking sad.

'We have caught Nathan stealing… yes Sir, yes, he says, engaging in conversation with my father.

'We are asking him to leave, yes for good', he says, answering my father's question.

My heart drops, WHAT THE FUCK, my dad is going to kill me. This can't be happening again. Maybe I should run, run away and live off the doll, but I'm too young. This system would never let a youngster like me live off the dole; they will make me go to some government school out in whoop whoop.

I'm fucked now, but at least I get to sleep in my bed watch my TV and eat good food, not to mention the weed that sits in Bondi waiting for me to arrive. Might not be so bad after all. I'll deal with dad's hour-long lecture, and he'll send me to my room where I'll get high and relax. Not so bad after all. Plus, I hate this place. I'll miss my new best friends but I'll see them this December holiday. Good fucking riddance to this place.

Brother Jeff puts down the phone. He looks at me and says 'You should have tried harder young man; apparently this was your last chance.'

'Last chance at what? What do you mean?' I ask both questions at the same time.

'Not sure young man, but your dad is fed up with you, he doesn't know what to do with you anymore. For many problem kids this is the end of the road. Nathan, I hope it's not the end for you.'

WHAT THE FUCK DO YOU MEAN, WHAT…? IS HE GOING TO THROW ME AWAY, I'M NOT A PIECE OF RUBBISH THAT YOU CAN JUST THROW AWAY. MAYBE THERE'S A PLACE THAT THEY SEND NAUGHTY KIDS LIKE MYSELF WHERE WE CAN

STAY FOREVER. 'Now go to your dorm and pack all your stuff and off you go.' As I'm walking out, Jeff says, 'Ill pray for you, Son. Good luck for the future. May God be with you.'

'What am I going to do with you now?' My dad speaks with a raised voice.

I take the 5th amendment, silence is golden.

'Hey, answer me, what do you want to do now? Or what are we going to do with you, because I'm all out of ideas?'

'I don't know Dad. I say sheepishly.'

And truth be told I really don't know. What I want and what he wants for me are two very different things.

I wish I could be honest with him.

DAD I WANT YOU TO LEAVE ME THE FUCK ALONE, PAY FOR MY WEED HABIT, AND LET ME SMOKE AS MUCH AS I WANT. I WANT TO GO TO THE BEACH EVERYDAY, GET HIGH AND DRUNK AND CHILL WITH MY FRIENDS. I DON'T WANT TO GO BACK TO SCHOOL, I HATE SCHOOL.

But I don't say that. 'I don't know Dad', is my choice of words.

The conversation dies, and an uncomfortable silence follows. 'I don't know Dad. I just don't know.'

Chapter 10

Being a dropout isn't that bad. I wake up to an empty house, in my big bed. There's twenty dollars sitting on the dining room table and the whole day is ahead of me, what a life.

As I descend the spiral stair case, I wonder what the boys are doing today. I feel like getting ripped and going for a surf, so I'll take my board down to the beach today.

I try to phone Adam's house, but there's no answer. Then Rubin and Dom. They must all be down at the beach already.

I eat my coco pops as fast as possible and run back upstairs. I begin to search my closet for my Bondi wear. I put on my Nautica shorts, my favorite Nike shirt and of course my deadly Air Max 95's. Not only am I one of the Bondi boys now but I also look the part. The last thing to go on is the Senate Kill Team flexi fit hat that I put on backwards. On my way out I grab the cash and a few coins that are left lying around. I need money for the bus.

I sit at the back of the bus, with my teckie (permanent marker) graffing up the sides, trying not to get caught by this bus driver. In Oz getting busted graffing is a big deal. The police here take it very seriously.

So I opt to graff up the seat. Finally we come around the last bend, down military road. The ocean view of Bondi is spectacular. South Bondi is littered with tourists and bathers. The waves at South Bondi for some reason are smaller than at North Bondi. The north is where it all goes down, surfing, the skate park in the north, and the spot where we all chill, get drunk and high. That spot sits right on the beach.

The waves have a glassy look in the sunlight. You can see the back spray as they break. I love the feeling of being down here. The girls are hot and topless, the beer flows like water and the weed smoke puts more clouds in the sky than God himself. This is where I would love to live when I can get

my own flat.

The bus arrives at my destination, right outside McDonald's. As I get out I see a few boys I know. Adam McGee, Chris, and Amin. No Matter who you're, McGee will rob, or at least hustle you for something. From experience I put the money down my pants, or he will try hustle me for half of it if not all of it. I walk over to say what's up, but as I arrive they turn and start running like nothing on earth. Very confused I almost break out into a sprint. Within seconds three cops run past me. One turns around and runs back up to me: 'Are you friends with those guys?'

'No why?', I ask, breaking out into a sweat.

'Never mind', he turns and runs after his butt buddies.

I better get down to the beach. Oh fuck! I left my board at home, so much for surfing.

I walk down the promenade, but it looks like not many people are at the skate park. Where the fuck is everyone? I stand on the top of the half pipe looking towards the beach, in search of my crew. Thoughts of where they could be rush around my head. They could be at Percy smoking it up, or they could be at the school, skating and graffing, or they could be in the junction, selling bud. Or maybe they're at Adam's spot smoking. I'll check Adam's joint first.

I knock; I can hear faint music coming out of the room. Someone must be here. Footsteps and then click, the door opens. It's Adam, and he looks different. It's his eyes. Usually they are all small and red, but today they are huge. I can't even see the colour of his eyes. He smells like alcohol and I can see he is highly strung, blinking a thousand times a second, licking his lips like a snake.

'What's up, what's up, what's up Bro? Give me a hug, come, come hug,' he says, rather fast.

I hug him, and as my head goes over his shoulder, I see my boy in the background -- Dom.

'What's up bro?', I say, having missed his company since I was expelled.

His eyes are duplicates of Adam.

'Not much Bro', you came right on time man.

He leans over and pulls out a large mirror, filled with about ten lines of what I suspect is cocaine.

'You got to try this coke Dude; it's the best shit I've ever blasted', Adam says, eyeing the goodies with desire, licking his lips like a maniac.

Mike hands me the cut in a half McDonald's straw. Then the mirror. Do these guys know that I've never done this before? I guess I just sniff and it's gone, consumed.

I prepare for the effects of his grade A drug.

I put the straw towards my nose. As I'm about to do the line, Adam says, very excitedly, 'Block your other nostril.'

I do so. The straw is in my nose and the second nostril is blocked. I've got butterflies but I'm excited to do this. The line starts disappearing as it goes into the straw, up my nose and into my brain. The feeling of powder sitting in my nose and throat is horrendous. I don't think any of it went to my brain. But just then it happens, the strong effects of the Blow take place. I might throw up. The effects are weird. It's not the unmanageable feeling that I thought It was going to be, its controlled. As the effects heighten something new happens. It's warm and fuzzy. I feel like a man, no seriously, like a real man. Strong powerful, confident, fucking unbelievable, unstoppable. I feel as if I just turned into GOD.

I sit back, light up a smoke and draw back on the nicotine. It's better than it's ever been, so satisfying. Adam pours me a drink and hands it over, pure vodka no chaser, no water, no lime and lemonade. I sip it and it tastes good, how the fuck did I live without this shit!

I motion towards the mirror, Mike nods. I sit forward and vacuum the pure white powder faster this time. I can't seem to get enough. I wonder if he'll care if I have two in a row. I switch nostrils and sniff like there's no Tomorrow.

Damn Bro slow down, you going to OD if you keep that up. Plus each line costs me twenty dollars, Dom says, looking rather concerned.

'Shit Bro, I've only got twenty dollars on me', I say now realizing I'm in debt.

'Don't worry man, this is my shout. I just ripped someone off and got a fair bit of cash.' So I bought two grams. This is only half of the first, so we got quite a bit to use, but we need to pace ourselves. I mean look at Adam, he's fucked.'

'What's wrong with him Dude? Why's he doing that stuff?'

I look at Adam. He runs to the windows, looks outside… then to the door to check its locked. Then he looks through the key hole… then back to the window. He repeats this process more and more the more lines he has.

Am I going to start acting mad soon? I wonder to myself.

I drain the glass of its contents. More and more I feel like a fiend.

I don't remember ever wanting something so bad. More alcohol, more coke, more cigarettes… more, more, more.

I sit back and watch a few clouds pass by the window …

Adam says he is going to the toilet. He is out the room faster than I can say cool.

Mike leans over to me and says: 'Dude we've got to get away from him… he could become dangerous.'

I nod, now becoming a bit scared of Adam and his unpredictable behaviour. 'I will spike his drink with two sleeping pills…,when he passes out,we will go', Mike says looking straight at me.

I nod.

Dom spikes the drink before Adam is out of the bathroom. Straight away Adam is at the window… then the door… then the window again before he sits down and knocks back the glass filled with straight vodka as if it was water. Dom smiles once it's down… thirty minutes and counting.

Within a few minutes the pills are taking effect. Adam is slowing down the intervals… The pauses between getting up to check the door are getting longer. He now drinks the vodka straight out the bottle. Twenty something minutes later, Adam's eyes close.

'You wanna go?' I ask Mike.

'I thought we should, but he'll sleep for a while as long as we don't make much noise, so we can chill here and finish the rest of the gram.'

'Good, I love this shit, except it's already wearing off… Why does it last for such a short time?'

Nathan Daniels

I think to myself: A drug as good as this should last for a lifetime. Yet I know life couldn't be that good. Everything good comes to an end eventually.

Meanwhile Mike puts the plate in the microwave. He heats it up before he puts the coke on its porcelain surface.

He then takes out his credit card and proceeds to assault the powder over and over again, crushing and sweeping it, crushing and sweeping. Poor beautiful magic powder. I think I'll call it "the miracle cure" that magic cure for self-esteem, impotence, whatever. I believe it will fix everything. They should give it to doctors for surgery, prostitutes for sex and lawyers for court cases.

My time has come. It's time to inhale the cure. I repeat the same process as before. Once again, the effects take place. God help me. Silence falls as I pour the remainder of the vodka into two small cups.

I might regret the next question, but I ask it anyway: 'Mike… earlier you said you ripped someone off, who might that someone be, and what did you rip off?'

Mike smiles. It's a smile that I've never seen before – a smile of guilt, anger, and sadness. I can't quite put my finger on that smile. Then he says,

'I know it might sound mad but I stole my mother's jewellery.'

He waits for my reaction. I say nothing, but I can see the reason for his tyranny. If I had known this substance existed, I would also steal anything from anyone.

Mike leans forward and puts the straw towards his nose. He sucks up the remainder of the pure white snow. He leans back on the couch, stares out the window. He's deep in thought, so I leave him to himself.

I do the same… I lean back, light a smoke. I fall deep into my twisted mind…

Fall from Grace

Thoughts. I wonder what is happening to me? I feel really good, but uncertainty lurks inside. I push it down. I open my eyes and look for the liquid exterminator. It's within range, so close to oblivion, but it never comes. It's not like I wanna die… I just want to feel something other than that feeling I felt at the airport…

'Mike do you have any bud?'

Mike opens his eyes. 'Ye Bro. You chop', he says, throwing me the stick.

As the bud hits my hand, a beautiful sense of calming relief falls upon the late afternoon sun…

Note to self: Just for this moment I feel perfect.

'Mike… it's chopped…'

Chapter 11

Sunday morning. Last night was heavy. I drank too much stout mixed with vodka and soda… a potent mixture, considering I smoked two joints and put about half a gram of Blow up my nose. The rest is quite blurry, so I won't embellish.

I walk out my bedroom, there's silence.

'Hello', I call out, hoping no one is home.

After a minute of silence a surge of energy runs through my hung-over body. I walk back into my room, grab my smokes and head out onto the balcony.

I light a smoke trying to think of the events of last night. I remember taxing a bit of the weed for this morning. I wonder where it is. It was a joint so it must still be in my smoke pack. I grab the pack again. As I open it, there sits the spliff. I walk into the adjacent room where my computer sits, and I open win amp. I put on Eminem and off I go to light the light of my life.

The greenery is over. The effects of the weed don't feel the same. A gram

would be lovely right now.

LIGHT BULB MOMENT. My parents are out. There are a number of things I can do.

Fall from Grace

1. Phone the parents.

   'Hi Mom, yeah, where are you guys?'

   'Okay, good stuff. I'm going to shower and go down to the beach. I'll speak to you later (...) Yes mom, I'll behave, bye.'

2. Go downstairs. Find the key to the naughty cabinet. Open the cabinet. Grab a great whiskey and have a drink.

3. Go back upstairs. Find some sort of drug to consume. Dad has a med's cupboard bigger than most pharmacies.

4. Search the rents room for cash to get some blow.

5. Finally, get the blow and sniff like today is my last day on earth.

My five simple steps to oblivion.

'Yes his phone is ringing... What's up Fucker, I got a huge score Bro!'

'What? Who did you do over?' Mike asks, sounding very interested.

'I'll tell you all about it. Let's meet in the junction.'

'Sweet Dude. How long?'

'Um... I'll get in a taxi right now. I'll be there in fifteen.'

'Sweet Bro', he says, now jumping around with joy.

I knew Dom would be waiting very eagerly for me at the entrance to the cinemas. We've risen above the scum of Bondi. Fuck McDonald's, fuck LBM and fuck all the life suckers that used me. We're civilized users, they're addicts. We stay in 5 star hotels while they sleep on the streets, we're different.

'What's up Dude?' Dom says, already looking high. His lips look licked to perfection.

'You wanna know bitch? Here'

I throw a wad of cash in hundred dollar bills towards Mike. It totals $3800.

He catches it and looks at it. He looks back at me, and then looks at it again. That fucking smile forms. He throws it back and laughs.

'So Dude, what would you like to do with this cash?' Mike asks (as if he knows my thoughts).

'First off all, let's get an ounce of weed and two grams of blow each', I say, now feeling like the leader of our small crew.

'Sweet… And I've got a place for us to go', Mike says.

It's six o'clock and I'm well and truly hammered, walking out of Anthony's massive Vaucluse house. Funny enough, I live literally around the corner. It's time to go home now. My rents don't know where I've been all day and I know they will be angry. I hope Dad doesn't realise the money is missing straight away, if he does. He has no proof that I took it. He never will. I'll hide it straight away. I'll put it in my undies when I arrive. Then I'll go hide it in my old school shoes, where I hide all my stash.

All the lights are on in the house. Maybe we have visitors. Act normal Nathan, stop clenching your jaw. No lip licking and don't talk to fast. Close your eyes a little. There we go now. I look normal. Ready to take on the world.

I push the door open, expecting to see lots of people, a dinner party in process. But it's not to be. My dad comes rushing forward.

'Where is it?' He asks with a look that sends shivers down my spine.

Lie Nathan lie. 'What? What you talking about?'

'The money, I know you took it, now where the fuck is it?'

'What money Dad?, I don't have money.'

What if he strips me and finds the cash? I truly believe he will kill me, literally.

I make my way past him, acting like I'm insulted that he'd dare accuse me of this heinous crime.

My dad goes into the lounge to talk things over with the rest of the family.

'Nathan come down here this instant', my mom calls out.

'Just wait, I can't deal with this shit. How can you guys accuse me of this?'

I shout out as convincing as possible.

I run into my room, open my cupboard. I grab the old school shoes and shove the remainder of the coke and cash into the small stash. I cover the shoes with more old shoes and turn to go confess my innocence.

'Nathan you're a fucking liar, we know you stole the money', my sister says.

'Fuck you Cara, you the one who has coke in your bag all the time', I say trying to blow her out the water and shift the attention off myself.

'Bullshit, Dad, he is so full of shit, I fucking hate him. Can't you guys see he is a drug addict?,

While I and my sister are arguing, my dad leaves the room.

Within minutes, he is back downstairs, holding my old school shoe. The cash and blow in his hand. 'Then what the fuck is this Nathan?' He asks this looking homicidal.

Nathan Daniels

OH MY GOD, HERE WE GO. Usually I can gage what my consequence will be, this time is different. This might really land me on the streets.

'So what now, how you going to deny it now?' My sister asks.

I've got no comeback. Tears fall down my face. The pain I've been drowning in drugs and alcohol comes out in waves. I feel like I might pass out. I've done the unthinkable. The guilt, shame and self loathing develop within seconds. A moment of clarity forms. But it's too late. 'You've got a serious problem, how could you do this to your family? You're a fuck up… a royal fuck up.' Just in case I had doubts, my father concurs. 'Idiot, rubbish, dog'…Many other words that I've forgotten.

Crying won't help, they're not going to say, 'Okay you look sorry, so it's okay.' This is going to go on for a long time. Tonight is only the start. The remainder of the night I sit deep in thought. What just happened…? I try work out why I do the things I do. I try justify my behaviour by blaming my family, and mainly my father. Deep inside I know that nothing on earth can justify my behaviour. I've got a serious problem, even though I don't want to stop drugs. I don't think I could. Throughout the night I think of ways to get high or drunk. Nothing comes to surface… Around the twilight hours, I fall into a light sleep. I'm not comfortable in my own bed or my own skin. Maybe I should tell them about my problem, maybe I shouldn't.

Ten o'clock the following day: My mom comes in to my room, and wakes me gently. For some reason she is the only one who understands. I love waking up -- there's that second before the thoughts start running. A moment of thoughtlessness, when my mind doesn't realise what it's done. It doesn't last for very long. Those revolting feelings flood in very quickly. I can see my mom has been crying, probably the whole night.

I fall apart at the seams. I want to die. I can't take this shame, this pain and this guilt.

'Don't cry Boy, we're going to help you. You going to a rehab, where they help people with problems like yours', my darling mother says, relieving the pain a little.

Finally a possible solution.

'Okay', I say, finding it impossible to look my hurting mother in the eyes.

Moms have a way of making the worst situation better with one word or one touch. My mom is my savior. Thank you God for blessing me with such an amazing person.

'Let's go Boy; pack a small bag. I'll makes you some breakfast and we'll go. You can have a nice break.'

'Okay, I'll do that, but I don't want breakfast', I say, getting out of my bed to begin the boring process of packing.

Something is wrong. My body hurts, it's not emotional hurt though. This is weird, I've never felt this before. I need to get high even though I really don't want to. It's the last thing on my mind but I want it. Or my body wants it. Maybe I'm just confused.

I pack my ridiculously small bag. I head to my bathroom to grab my toiletries. I'm ready to go not really expecting anything out of this holiday I'm embarking on.

'Mom, how long is the drive?'

'About an hour, if there's no traffic.'

'An hour? Where the fu… hell is this place?'

'It's called North Side Clinic, so I guess it's on the north' she says, looking rather irritated by all my questions. Pity I'm just getting started.

'Okay, so what do we do there?'

'Well they've got groups, counseling, a gym, pool table and TV. You get your own room. It sounds very nice.'

Okay that sounds okay, now for the million dollar question.

'How long am I going for?'

'It's a 28 day programme Boy, but they have options. There are places you can go after, if you feel like you want to carry on with the programme, as they call it, not sure what programme it is but I guess we'll see.'

'I change the radio station and by divine grace Tupac's song changes is on.' *I wake up in the morning and I ask myself is live worth living should I blast myself...* that's exactly how I feel this morning.

We arrive at a very modern building with the words NORTH SIDE CLINIC sprawled across it.

Note to self: This really doesn't look so bad after all; I might want to continue on after this.

Plus I'm almost fifteen, maybe I can just take a break and everything will go back to the way it was at the beginning. That would be nice... no reason to steal any more, no more sleepless nights. I mean, I can't even eat without being stoned anymore. I need a change or a break... whatever you call it, as long as after this, things will go back to normal.

'Mom, I might actually enjoy this place...'

Chapter 12

I walk into this modern building, expecting the worst. All the tales of rehab, abuse and groups involving people shouting at you about how bad you are, seem like the furthest thing from the truth.

This looks like a mixture between a health spa and a hospital.

My mother and I take a seat on some very comfortable chairs.

Note to self: The only problem is that I still have the hunger. No it's not a hunger for food, it's a hunger for something that will make this situation easier.

My hands sweat and my body aches. Maybe I'm getting sick, flu'ey perhaps, who the fuck knows? What do I do? I know my mind is very specific about what it wants: A swimming pool full of glorious whiskey, a bath full of pink Peruvian marching powder, and of course the good old trusty plant, that God clearly made for smoking.

We are greeted by a young pretty woman, named Sue.

'Hi Nathan, Fiona, my name is Sue. I'm the medical director of the clinic.

Please come in to my office.'

She has a fake Picasso on the wall and those same nice chairs at her desk.

'So' Sue asks, 'how can I help you?'

Nathan Daniels

My mom answers first, 'Um... you see sue Nathan is obviously very young, and we understand you don't usually take people as young as Nathan, but we're in a critical situation and we don't know how to get out of it. We desperately need your help.'

'Okay, I see. Nathan do you honestly want to stop using?'

I look at the floor and nod. Suddenly feeling very insecure.

'Okay, Fiona, why don't you leave Nathan and myself alone so we can discuss what happens here and see what he would like out of us?'

Immediately my mom gets up and leaves. Within seconds I'm alone with this young, hot doctor.

'So Nathan, how you feeling right now?'

'Um... not great, I think I might be getting the flu.'

She stares into my eyes and says: 'Tell me exactly what you feeling.'

Here we go: 'I feel like I'm starving but I'm not hungry. I feel like I want to get lost and never be found. My heart is beating so fast that it might burst. My hands are sweating, but I'm cold. I'm confused and angry.'

'Okay, why are you angry?'

'Honestly?' I ask. It's about to get very real:

'Well I stole alot of money from my dad. It was his fault anyway for leaving it around in such a stupid place, anyone could have found it. Plus, I don't really know why I took it. You see I knew what I was doing was wrong, but I did it anyway. It felt like I couldn't really help myself, and this causes the confusion; the anger is mainly anger towards myself for...'

Tears begin to well up... 'losing control or feeling like I'm losing control...'

Tears fall...

'I don't know why I do what I do. What I do know is I love what drugs do for me.'

'First of all, Nathan, what drugs does a youngster like yourself do?'

'Um...' Should I be honest? Should I tell her everything? Why not, it won't hurt to tell her.

'Cocaine, weed, alcohol and occasionally sleeping pills.'

She nods while writing my info on a piece of paper. Then she says, 'Wow, and how old are you?'

'Fifteen', I say, realizing the absurdity of this situation.

She stares for a moment, and then says, 'Okay we don't usually take people of your age. Well we don't usually take people under eighteen, but at your age, using the drugs you use, I don't think you'll live till eighteen.'

'You need to understand that your body isn't even almost finished developing. The damage you do now, will change the way your body grows and develops. It's five times more dangerous for you to use drugs than let's say for an adult of thirty.

'Nathan I just hope two things: One, you're not too far gone into addiction. Two, that you realise the seriousness of this situation, because it's very serious.'

'So what would you like from us?'

'Again to be honest, I really don't know. I don't know what happens here. I don't know what's wrong with me... so how could I know what to do?'

'Okay, Nathan, I see your confusion. Well we will take you for the 28 day programme and discuss your process along the way. Are you ready to come in now?'

'Yes I am, I got my bag in the car.'

'Okay good, now go outside and tell your mom to come in. I would like to tell her what's happening. You can go get your bag. Take it through to the nurses' station just down the hall and they will show you to your room and take you through and show you around the residential area. You see there's a general area, then there's a psychiatric ward and a drug ward. One of the biggest rules is, don't go into the other wards. Some of the people in the psych ward are dangerous. So no going in there, okay?'

'Yep, no problem', I say, walking out of the office looking for my mother dearest.

'Mom, she wants me to go get my bag and take it in down there', I say, pointing at the longest passage I've ever seen.

'Okay here', she hands me the keys to her car, 'Go get the bag and I'll meet you down there.'

I'm now walking down this long hallway. I pass the psych ward, which has a door that looks bullet proof and crazy people proof. It really does look scary.

I get to a door that doesn't look quite as thick as the psych ward's door, but it still looks scary.

I ring the bell, and the door opens within minutes.

Standing before me is a nurse. She looks like the splitting image of the doctor except she's in a cute outfit. She makes my pants tingle.

'Hi young man, who are you coming to visit?'

'No-one, I'm coming to stay here for a while.'

She giggles, 'No really, Sally is your mum isn't she?'

'Who's Sally? My mum's name is Fiona, and seriously I'm here to stay.'

'Okay, well come with me', she says as she grabs my pathetic little case dropping it in the nurses' station, 'I'll show you around, and then I'll show you to your room. Just wait here for one second', she points to a room with a few couches.

'Okay', I say, walking towards the room.

This room is lush; the couches in here are like futons, soft, bedlike. I like this couch...

'Nathan, first let me show you to your room, then I'll show you around.'

We enter a small but comfortable room, with a single bed, decent bed covers, a small bathroom with a shower, and a desk with a good wooden chair.

'Now this will be your room for your whole stay, it's not much, but I'm sure it will do.'

'Yeah, it's not bad at all', I say, not lying.

'Okay now let me show you around, this place is quite big, so try keep up.'

'Nathan, its medication time', some random nurse says approaching me.

Thank fuck because I was starting to worry. As I said before, my body is going though some horrible shit. It's a very weird desire, an obsession I would call it. My mind doesn't stop thinking about blow... that sweet, sweet, soft powder... so pretty, yet so painful. I fucking love it!

I wonder what goodies I'm going to be getting? Tranq's, sleepers,uppers, downers, or adding abit of hunter S Thompson, laughers or screamers? I don't give a fuck. As long as they mess me up enough to sleep, then all is well.

I walk to the nurse's little window. A definitely gay nurse stands behind the desk. There's an array of medications in little see-through cups. It looks like my sort of party behind there.

'Name?' He asks in a thick Irish accent.

'It's Nathan, it's my first day.'

'Okay. Here you take these at this counter. Once you've swallowed them, you must show me your mouth, so I can see they are down. Understand?'

Yes I understand these very simple instructions you just gave me. I might be young but I'm not stupid, I think to myself.

'Yep, that's fine.'

I gulp the pills down, with haste. Very excited about where this is going and effects await me.

I go sit outside in the court yard to have my last smoke before bedtime. I've been informed by the rather gay nurse that these pills will make me very unstable, and that I should not walk around.

Whatever Dude. You obviously have no idea how much toxin I pump into my body. I'm a fucking soldier.

Suddenly I get a whiff of the unmistakable smell of the chronic (weed).

It has to be… my nose is like a blood hound for that shit. I get up and walk around the edges of the porch. It's strongest by the back building where I'm not allowed to go. I must be going mad. I'm in rehab. No one smokes around rehabs. I go sit back at the table telling myself to chill the

Fall from Grace

fuck out. This isn't real. Maybe the pills are kicking in. Maybe my mind is playing tricks on me. I don't know, but I'm sure it was real. I throw my smoke into the bushes even though there's an ashtray right in front of me.

As I'm getting up to leave, a hobbling figure comes out of the darkness. It's that heavy junkie-looking chick with no teeth. For a moment I thought it was a ghost. I almost shat myself. Fucking junkies.

'Hey man, you got a smoke I can bum?', she asks, while the smell of chronic surrounds me as she speaks.

'Yeah no problem', I hand her a smoke, thinking of how I'm going to ask her if she has been smoking.'

I ask outright as we sit in silence, 'Have you been smoking?'

'Smoking what honey?', she asks with her rough voice and missing teeth.

'You know', I lean forward so no-one hears me, 'Weed?'

'Hahaha'... she laughs and releases more of the beautiful fumes. 'Maybe I have.'

'I can smell you badly…, I could smell it while you were smoking back there.'

'Okay youngster', she says, 'I've been smoking and if you keep quiet, Tomorrow my man is bringing me more, and you can join my party if you want.'

'Cool, definitely I would love to smoke', I now say excited.

'Okay well it's on then', she says, throwing her smoke in the same place I did. Great minds think alike I guess, the pills are definitely kicking in now, everything is slowing down, oblivion is fast approaching. 'Nice, I better get to my room.'

I fall onto the soft mattres in slow motion. I can feel the pillows exhale as my heavy head falls upon them. The blanket is cozy and warm. I really do like this place after all. 28 days of luxury and weed is not a bad combination. I stumble to the toilet. This feeling is unstable, I can barely hold it together. My mood is retarded and unpredictable… I piss all over the floor and the lid of the toilet.

I better go to bed before I do more damage… Goodnight cruel world.

Chapter 13

Myself and the deranged junkie, Jules, have grown careless. We crouch in the corner of the court yard.

I light the joint and look around. I turn towards her because she is now standing staring straight at the gay nurse, who is standing right in front of me. He peers at my hand as the weed smoke wafts towards his nose.

GOD DAMN, I never get away with anything anymore.

'Nathan, you know the rules. This is completely unacceptable, you're endangering other peoples' lives here, unlike you and Jules here. Some people actually want to stop using and by you bringing that stuff in here you make it unsafe for them.'

Maybe its the pills or the frustration of me getting caught before I got high that makes me flip out. This is what happens:

'YOU KNOW WHAT, YOU FUCKNG FAGOT? CALL MY FAMILY OR THE COPS, I DON'T GIVE A FUCK ANYMORE.'

'Excuse me?' he asks walking up to me.

'YOU HEARD ME, YOU'RE A FAG, I DON'T LIKE YOU OR THE WAY YOU LOOK AT ME. WHAT YOU GOING TO DO FAIRY? YOU GONNA HIT ME?'

Nathan Daniels

'No Nathan I'm not going to hit you, you're a little junkie, whose opinion matters as much as my dogs. You're nothing, you never going to be anything. YOU GOING TO DIE WITH A FUCKING NEEDLE IN YOUR ARM and you know the saddest thing? Nobody gives a fuck.'

I got nothing to say. Nice comeback but it means nothing. I couldn't possibly sink any lower than this. Just another fuck up to add to my resume.

THREE DAYS LATER…

I've gone into full destructive mode. Fuck my family, fuck my life. I want out. In order for me to get away from this fucking tragic failure of a family, I need enough money to…

1. Pay for a couple of months' rent in a shithole flat.
2. Be able to buy enough drugs to deal and use.
3. Party up a storm.

I see my mom's bag next to her bed. She is in the bath. There won't be enough money in her purse for my departure, but there will be credit cards and ATM cards.

I reach in to her bag, take out the purse. Am I actually going through with this?

Fuck it; take all the cards and bounce.

I do so. I walk toward my room. Open the balcony door, throw my back pack off the balcony and follow suit. I'm free. Finally, I'm free. No rules or regulations. It's me and lots of money and the freedom to do whatever it is I want to do. One big word comes to mind: DRUGS AND LOTS OF THEM.

I run to the closest ATM, and draw out the limits. $1000 a card. Three cards $3000. Enough to do all the things I want for a couple of days at least. I call on a few of my friends.

Fall from Grace

We land up in a hotel room with a case of beer, twenty white lacostes, an ounce of the best blow I could find and of course the old trusty plant that has been there since the start of my secret love affair.

Days roll into nights, nights into days. People come and people go but one thing stays the same. I'm alone. No Matter how many people there are around me, I still feel lonely.

I sit on the balcony, waiting for an answer. For once in the two days I'm alone. No one here except me, my drugs and my twisted thoughts.

Should I go home? I can't… those bridges have been burnt. Dad would take the cards that don't even work anymore and kick me out into the street.

Fuck, I'm going to be a bum. Plus this is his fault.

Should I kill myself? I drop another pill and sip it down with a beer. Stick my hand into the fine white powder, fuck lines. I sniff the remainder of the powder off my hand.

Tears begin to fall. WHAT THE FUCK IS WRONG WITH ME?, I'M FIFTEEN AND I JUST BECAME HOMELESS.

I lie on the bed. I'm slipping in and out of sleep. I'm restless, irritable, hungry and cold. I'm praying and begging God to save me. Take me God. Take me away from this place. Make things right.

Just then, a knock on the door. It should be Dom. I wipe my eyes and open the door. Oh shit.

'Marat, Dean what you guys doing here?'

(These Russians are big and scary, mobsters most likely)

'Nathan, you're in trouble. Your sister is downstairs waiting for you. It's over. We found you. We are now taking you home', Marat says, looking friendly.

I say 'Okay', and a sense of relief falls over me. I'm fucked but thank God this situation is over.

I drop two more pills as we walk towards my sister's car. Her eyes are swollen from crying I suspect. We all climb into her car. Words are not needed. I know Cara is hurting.

She then says, 'Nathan we're going to Diamond bay to talk about this.'

'Okay', I say, not suspecting anything.

Marat, Dean and I walk off to a bench. Cara said she'll be there in a minute. Marat asks for the cards. I willingly hand them over. I light a smoke.

Out of the blue Marat hits me. It's not a love tap or a slap, but a full fisted closed hand punch right under my eye. The sheer size of his fist and strength sinks me straight away; blood runs into my mouth and eyes. I slip out into darkness but not before I beg Marat to stop kicking me, while Dean is also kicking my face and head.

I come to, at the front of our house. Cara's crying and saying sorry. The pain is agonizing, my one eye is closed. My lip is split, and as I breathe, my body hurts. My body is riddled with welts and instant bruises.

Note to self: This can't be real. How could they do this to me?

My family… My family… How can they do this to me? My family… Once again… the very people who are meant to protect me and save me are betraying me.

My dad opens the front door. Marat stands behind.

'Jesus', he says, looking shocked. He hits me to top it all off, 'Go clean yourself up.'

I walk up the stairs as Marat and father sort out the payment I suspect. Nice Dad, you better lock your door tonight, because I'm going to slit your throat, you fucking prick.

I enter my bathroom to check the damage.

I'm shocked by what I see. My blood stained Helly Hanson jacket is ruined, my lip is completely split open, and my eye looks irreparably damaged. The bumps on my head look like ping pong balls. I lift off my shirt, to reveal a battered body of a young fifteen year old.

Fuck this, I'm seriously going to kill my father tonight. I fucking hate him with every inch of my soul. He is a failure of a man and of a father. Cockhead.

I walk past my mom's room. 'Nathan come here, she shouts.'

I turn and walk into her room. She gasps at the sight of me.

'Yeah, I know Mom, and you know what? Fuck you as well… you Fuckers better lock your door tonight, because I'm going to kill Dad… I'm going to… the remainder of the sentence I shout: SLIT HIS FUCKING THROAT, I shout as I'm walking towards my room.

'Nathan!!!' my father shouts out.

'FUCK YOU!!!' I shot back, 'Come near this room tonight and you'll cease to breathe… do you understand me!!!?

I slam my door and lock it for the night. I still have maybe two grams of blow left, twelve pills and a small amount of weed.

I think of all the ways to off my father and probably my fucking sister as well. My mom is still my angel and I believe she had nothing to do with this. So she will survive her slaughtered family.

The plan goes as follows: I quietly sneak out my room, downstairs to the alcohol cabinet. I remove the most expensive whiskey. I take a huge swig; the whiskey burns my broken lips. I go back into my room, to consume the fine brew.

I inhale multiple lines; light a smoke. Now I'm ready. I walk straight into my rents' room, smash the bottle on the wall, and with the sharp shards I begin the relentless motion of cutting my dad's head off.

Fuck this, I would never do that to him; he is my dad after all. But he needs to know how fucking hurt I am. Something like this will put a scar on our relationship forever. Writing this now at the age of 26 I can see the reasons for it. Being hopeless and angry does strange things to people.

I cry, snort and laugh deep into the night. I haven't slept in a few days. Flashes of true insanity show up. I'm talking to myself, laughing and staring into the mirror. I'm taking all my clothes off, and dragging a knife across my skin, I snort hatred, smoke, hatred, blood, lust, greed, more and more…

I fucking can't stop this disease. I can't stop this pain. I can't stop this hatred. I can't look in the mirror without bringing the blade to my throat.

What no one knows is this is the night I learnt the power of the blade.

Sitting in my death pit, I hold a knife in case those Fuckers come back. Someone as disturbed as me, in the situation I'm in, should never be near sharp objects.

The loathing, guilt and pain get too much, so I sink the blade deep into my arm. It hurts like nothing on earth, but it relieves the pain. I cut multiple wounds until the blood soaks my bed. I fall into a horrible delusional sleep, and nightmares I could never even mention come to my mind.

Fall from Grace

THIS NEEDS TO END. Suicide isn't an option. I need to get help.

I wake up, not sure of the time. My watch was lost in the scuffle last night.

I get off my blood stained bed, aching in ways I could never have dreamed of. Every breath I take in aches. My ribs are a deep purple. I can barely open my mouth because my lip has scabbed. I walk out my room, still not being able to see out my eye.

I want to just shout, 'HELP ME'. But my mom will think I'm being murdered.

I walk into her room; my dad has already gone to work.

'Mom please, I really need help', I say, crying now. 'Please, I'll do anything.'

'Okay relax' she says softly two hours later, trying to hide her tears. 'Your father found the best rehab in Sydney, we going at 8:30 to get you admitted.'

Addiction seems to be very confusing. On the one hand there's nothing more I want than to stop the cycle, but the FEAR is too great. It feels like knowing that the relationship you're in is unhealthy or just plain painful and you kind of brush it off hoping it will somehow get better. Yet, deep down in your heart, you know it has to end at some stage… and then there are those moments that remind of the reason you got together in the first place.

The relief is so huge, I almost faint. I stumble and then I fall.

I cry like I've never cried before. This feeling is so painful, yet so good at the same time.

Back in my room, wiping the tears away, I make the decision to use for the last time.

I take out the mirror from under my bedside pedestal, and rack the rest of the coke into two lines. I snort it, like it was the last time... Oh yeah, it is the last time.

Four pills left, I throw them down. I smoke the two bongs I got left, and then I throw the mirror and bong onto the road.

I feel quite proud of myself for this. I mean, I do realise I got a major problem. I just don't know how to deal with it. Hopefully going to this place being fully ready will help. Let's give it a shot, why not?

We pull up outside another modern building. SYDNEY CLINIC written across it. It looks okay. I don't really care but I need to get help.

Treatment is running alot smoother here. I've grown to love this place. I've learnt so much about this disease. I really think I might be able to stay clean.

I say my goodbyes to the nurses and a couple of people that I regard as friends. I leave the clinic with a bag full of meds. I'm now on anti-depressants and mood stabilizers. When I get stressed, I just take this little yellow pill, Valium, and it calms me down. So I got a solution to all my problems.

Once I'm home, the best fucking news comes to the surface.

A situation that I've been in before unfolds: The family is gathered. My dad and mom stand in front of my sister and I. Then the exciting news is broken:

'We are going back to South Africa.'

I burst out into tears, now being a very sensitive recovering drug addict, this is normal for me.

My sister is shocked, she doesn't say much.

My mom smiles. I know she hates it here almost as much as I do. FUCKING HELL, ALMOST FOUR YEARS, so much for the two year deal we had Dad.

I run up stairs. Thank God, I'm going home!!!

Chapter 14

Arriving back in Jozi was the biggest relief I had felt yet: My friends, my family and my school. Things would surely go back to normal now, no need or desire to put chemicals back into my body.

I'm greeted at the airport by my mom's brother and his lovely family. Also, I'm greeted by my best friend, Amy, who has been around since nursery school. She's been my longest friend ever. I'm overjoyed to see her.

This situation is abit overwhelming, but no Matter. I remove my rescue pills from my pocket. I never go anywhere without them. I take two pills and smile. Thank God I'm home.

Apparently, we're staying at my uncle's house while my mom looks for a house for us.

It's the end of November. All my friends are at school and are studying for exams so I get to say hello to them but that's it. It's fucking boring in Jozi not having the beach. I now have to rely on people to take me where I want to go. No more buses or trains. My independence has been stripped, but I guess it's just a small price to pay for the happiness I'm experiencing being back in the motherland.

Things are very different here. There is a lot more money at my disposal. Alcohol is freely available to my age group. The illegal activity here is rife, so to a using addict it's a haven. The number plates don't lie.

GP clearly stands for gangster's paradise.

Fall from Grace

My memories of the South Africa I lived in were false. The secure shell I had grown up in was gone. The family was not the same. My group of friends had changed, and my popularity status has been forgotten. My crazy stories of drugs, women, hotel rooms and rehab were frowned upon. My cool bad ass legacy was left behind in Australia. No one in Jozi thought I was cool for what I had done.

Soon after we arrived my mom had to go back to Australia to help my dad and granny. I was left alone. My aunt and uncle were busy working every day. I had the perfect recipe for a disastrous relapse.

And that's what happened. It starts off the same. I go score a matchbox full of Zol. It lasts me a week.

The next weekend, I'm drinking at Rosebank and smoking a joint. My drinking goes back to its usual pace. When everyone goes to sleep, I raid the alcohol cabinet. I don't drink because I enjoy the taste, but I drink for the effects: I drink to pass out, I drink because it makes me feel alive.

Eventually mom comes back and we move into a beautiful flat in Hyde Park. My relapse is still semi-secret. I think they know I'm drinking, but I'm covering it with 'All my friends are drinking, I only drink with them.' And it was shrugged away, that simple.

After a few months of being back at my old school, I start chilling with some of my old friends and I slowly start falling deeper and deeper into my pit of darkness.

My dad comes to see us, before his apparent move back.

Just then it happened. Not sure how it was done but my dad served my mom divorce papers. My poor mother's world fell apart. She landed up crying for days and eventually had a nervous breakdown. She ended up in hospital completely incapacitated. My sister and I were home alone for ten days. Cara is six years my senior. She has been affected by my behaviour but she also has a life. I couldn't expect her to look after me. Luckily it was in the December holidays so I didn't have to go to school. I was left alone most of the time. My

Nathan Daniels

mom had a very impressive med's cabinet. By the time my mom got home it was bare. I took everything, not really knowing what I took. Also, I had some shocking side-effects. One morning I had a sort of seizure from two pills. That wasn't nice.

I landed up in rehab again. My poor mom had way too much to deal with, so I was happy to give her a break. Well, my using was far from over.

In a Houghton house, I was back with like-minded people. I got an education of a different kind. I learnt about Hillbrow, Nigerians and of course the inevitable heroin and crack. People raved on about the unfucking believable effects of both. So I had to try it.

My first experience. Heroin was the next level. Jump on the gear, and you progress to a state of near death. It never fails to completely destroy everything around you. Try it, and you will sell all your family's valuables. And you will land up on the streets selling your body. GO HEROIN!!!

I went to Hillbrow to meet my new dealer, Max…

'Yo Max', I say, approaching the six foot, 150 kg African man.

'Hey White Boy, what you need?'

Note to self: Fine choice of words Max, you're right it's a need.

'You got some of that fine white powder you gave me last time?', I ask, looking around the deadly streets of the Brow.

'Sure sure my man, give me cash, I go get it', the hustler says to me.

I hand over 300 rand cash. I sit on the curb and wait for my dealer to return.

I try take in these surroundings. I'm totally not used to this amount of poverty, pain and disgrace. There's a vibe in the Brow that draws me in

Fall from Grace

but at the same time it freaks me out. This vibe keeps me at a safe distance. People every day come into the Brow and never leave. It's dark, cold and like blood infused water… scary. There are sharks here, big fucking sharks, waiting for small little white Jewish blood to spill.

The buildings are derelict. There's washing hanging over the balconies, and plastic covers on broken windows. This is definitely a place I don't want to land up in.

I see Max in the distance. My stomach starts getting soft… by that I mean I need a poo. My heart starts beating double time while my mind focuses on one thing: Oblivion.

'Everything sweet?' I ask, now dying for the toilet.

He says 'Yes, no. you see my brother, there's no coke here, we only have crack or Thai'.

'I don't want crack, but Thai sounds okay… but I'm not sure what it is or how to do it' I say to my trusty friend.

Hahaha', he laughs. Smirking with that evil look in his eyes. His response leaves me cold and shivering.

'My brother this stuff is cheaper than coke, I got you two grams.'

'Two grams, awesome my man.'

I take the two bags, thank my caring Nigerian friend and head back home.

Once I get home, I say hi to everyone. I'm very excited about this new drug. I go into the bathroom to sniff a line.

I unravel the plastic to reveal an off-white flaky substance. I whip out my gym card and organize a small line on the toilet lid.

Nathan Daniels

I steady myself for my first taste of heroin.

I do the line and almost immediately I start feeling the very, very powerful effects of the gear. An urge to lie down over comes me. Then comes the most unbelievable nausea that gets worse every time I move.

What the fuck is going on here? Max sold me a dud. But as I say this to myself, the real effects kick in place. The fucking feeling is far beyond anything in this world. I'm faced with the gates of heaven: God himself just touched my fucking soul. I fall back on the floor in complete ecstasy. There are no words to describe the feeling this is giving me. Fuck orgasms, fuck friends, fuck family, this is it. This is what I've been looking for my whole life.

I remember laying on the bathroom floor conjuring up all the most painful memories and images I can, but still I felt nothing. I thought of the rejection of losing my father to some strange women and some other family. I feel he left us because his little fucking plan of this immigration failed. Not only did it fail but his whole family and life fell apart, so I believe he ran away, exchanged his failure of a family for a new productive family. I haven't even met them but I hate them. I'm under the suspicion that he hooked up with her before my mother and him were divorced. God help him if I find out that he has done that. But whatever, the bottom line is he's a product of history, he doesn't know any better. So fuck it, I guess it lands on me to break the running away father chain. I would never do to my family. I would never do what my father has done to us.

I need to go to my bed right now. I sit up and vomit again but who cares about vomit when it makes you feel this good. I wrap up the goodies and stand, vomit. I unlock the door, make my way to my room, close the door and fall onto my soft big bed. I vomit into the bin next to my bed every ten, fifteen minutes. I lie there, not being able to move, speak or flinch. I'm caught up in the godliness of this situation.

Heroin has unbelievable effects on my body. I love the feeling more than I've loved anything in my life. This drug has shown me something I never knew existed. What it's really done, is numb my body and mind beyond anything I've ever used. The constant mental suicide thoughts are gone. Not dulled but absolutely gone. FUCK, YES, THIS IS IT! I'VE FOUND THE SOLUTION.

THANK GOD FOR HEROIN.

Chapter 15

When you get to a stage where heroin has become a serious problem (I mean when heroin becomes your life force), then you basically do whatever it takes to get the next bag.

By this stage of my using career, I no longer cared what anyone thought about my using. I still tried to hide my using from my mom but I wasn't that bothered if she found out that I was using. I'm pretty sure she did know that I was drinking every day and smoking weed, but no-one knew that heroin had became such a big part of my life. Not even my then long-term girlfriend, Stacey.

One fine day, no one was home and I was running around the house looking for money or something to sell. All I had to use was shitty weed, which by this stage wasn't enough to keep me from getting sick. All my accounts at the bottle store were in excess and the dealer would never let me get anything on credit. I still owed him R500 from two days ago, so the last resort was to steal. I was going through the library/computer room and I came across a rather long key. Instantly I knew where it was from -- the safe. At the time I didn't know that the safe held all my mom's jewellery but within ten minutes I knew just how much jewellery it contained. And so the internal battle began. Do I steal something small? Maybe just small gold pieces? Or do I leave it?

Note to self: How the fuck can you steal from someone like your mom who has given you everything in this world?

How can you steal from the one who has looked after you since you were born? The one who adopted you and gave you a life that only exceeded your understanding of what a life should be like? The one who loves you more than she loves herself? The one who sacrificed her marriage and her life for her dear son who has fucked up everything beyond comprehension? I'M SO SORRY MOM.

The internal battle had begun. I closed the safe and put the key away. I then went back into my room, smoked a bong and lay down. The cramps had started and I knew it was only the start of this hideous process. I started walking back towards the safe room and turned around. I CAN'T DO THIS. I MUST DO THIS. I'M GOING TO GET SICK IF I DON'T DO THIS. FUCK, I CAN'T DO THIS TO OUR FAMILY. I went back to my room again, slammed the door and jumped on the bed. I then screamed into a pillow. Eventually the battle was lost and the desire to end the sickness won. I stole a diamond ring.

Once I started the binge of all binges I was lost inside the desire for destruction and oblivion. My day to day activity was wake up, throw up in the bin next to the bed, and try to get brandy or vodka down (which usually ended up with more vomiting). Then I would try get a bit of heroin down, which also usually ended in dry heaving. It would take a few attempts to get any sort of substance down, then blood shot eyes and a deathly smell would engulf the room. Yet I didn't care. I would light a smoke and then just lay there, wondering what next. Where do I go from here? Usually it would involve getting up and heading to the kitchen to drink something other than the toxic fucking soul stealing liquid that littered my room. I would ask Rose to make me coffee. I would go sit on the patio and act like I was actually okay, when in reality I was a total fucking mess. Who the fuck wakes up and vomits like six times before even getting out of bed? Who does this and then attempts to watch the 7 o'clock news? Watching the news so pissed that I couldn't even focus my eyes properly. The next part of the day usually revolved around getting back into the room and continuing on this path of destruction: drink, drunk, gulp, inhale, pass out, wake up, puke, smoke, and sniff, and drink, drunk, gulp and so on.

This type of lifestyle was not acceptable to my mom and sister and I would often go on drunken rages when they confronted me about the drinking. I broke windows and punched a whole straight through the huge front door to the house.

There's something that used to happen that to this day I feel so fucking guilty about: My mom would be down for the count, laying in bed with all sorts of tears and sore stuff happening to her because her son is busy killing himself. And somewhere along the line, we would have huge fights, where I would say such horrible things like 'I don't blame Dad for divorcing you. All you do is lie in bed and cry, you're useless.' Then, one time I crossed the line and said I wish she never adopted me. From my side and from hers this was the blade that properly cut us, deep down to the core.

The second last day of using was when everything came down: I had been drinking all day and I was horribly drunk when a friend came and said he wanted to go out and chill. So we went, and little did I know my sister had phoned him and told him to come get me out the house. When I was gone my sister and mom went through all my stuff and when I returned, I was confronted by them. They had found some jewellery under my bed. I really didn't remember taking what she had, but she went through her safe and found out all I had taken. The small destructive world I had set up was now crashing down all around me. The guilt and shame came to a head, just like a pimple it had been building and building and finally someone popped it. I fucking lost my mind, I hadn't ever felt so bad, like my soul was defective. I had seriously just fucking become the disgusting piece of shit that I thought I was. There was only one option in this all, SUICIDE!!!

So I went into my room, locked the door and prepared for the inevitable. I cut myself and so clichéd, I wrote a suicide note in blood. The next series of events are muddled up and confusing. As I said, earlier I was by that stage a blackout drinker. I drank as much as I could swallow. I know that a policemen was called. I smashed all my cupboard doors off and threw my TV against the wall. The destruction had reached a new level. I woke up the next morning or sometime during the evening and there was blood all over the bed. I had pieces of glass in my wrist. I had savagely torn open my wrists with a broken tot glass.

The next leg of the tour was Cape Town.

Chapter 16

Natasha Sharon. Sometimes I believe in the back of my mind that she was the one I should have stayed with. In hindsight, our relationship was based on dishonesty and lust. It had nothing to do with wanting to be together for the purpose of an actual relationship. She was what I'd call my first love, well she was the first real girlfriend I ever had when I was sober and clean. I guess that made the feelings seem stronger. Anyway, Natasha and I had quite a long history together before we actually became boyfriend and girlfriend.

I met Natasha at a Jewish camp thingy called Habonim. I had just returned from Sydney and instead of spending the time with my family, I opted to go on the camp, which was probably the best idea since I had a fucking ball. Anyway while we were setting up our tents, there were these Cape Town girls setting up their tent behind us. Almost instantly I took a liking to Natasha. She was beautiful, confident and bitchy. I don't know what it's about girls that have an attitude, but I'm very attracted to that sort of thing.

One night Natasha and I were sitting around the fire having a smoke. With my thick Australian accent I asked if I could kiss her. Words were not spoken. Lips meshed, hands touched and just like that Natasha became my camp girl. Sadly this wasn't meant to last. In those days I was quite a player and after two or three days, I was kissing someone else and she had moved on too. We did remain friends though. Eventually I was kicked out of the camp for hitting someone in the face. What was really weird was that Natasha was crying her eyes out because I was leaving and my own chick didn't really seem to care.

Nathan Daniels

I had got in contact with Natasha some time later again when smoking weed with one of her friends one night. The time came when we would meet up at the Valve, a night club in Sea Point. It just so happened that it was my seventeenth birthday that night. The only problem (which wasn't really a problem) is that I was with a girl named Stacey at the time, but Stacey wasn't in Cape Town for another two days. The alcohol mixed with the weed and the fact that we had unfinished business was just way too much to bear. The minute I saw Natasha standing outside the club, I knew it was on, she was fucking gorgeous, like seriously fucking gorgeous. Inside the club we danced and drank and then it happened… the moment that no mortal man could have resisted. We went outside to grab some fresh air as they say. There was that moment when I knew a kiss was coming and then as predicted it came. The feeling overtook us. We were locked in each other arms for a few hours after. Then, just as fast as it came, that feeling, tension and mood left.

I'm nineteen and in rehab in Cape Town. I had been in treatment for almost five months now. Old Dr Lancaster is here to visit me. He takes me out for the day. We go to the beach as Cape Town has some really beautiful beaches. Today we decide to go to Clifton 4th beach. While lying on the hot sand, two girls walk past. I look at them and tell my dad to look at those chicks. I'm trying to initiate some sort of father son perving session. At this moment the one turns around and looks in my direction. What do you know? It's Ms Natasha Sharon. Looking as fine as hell. I walk over and greet her, and right away I know I'm staying in Cape Town. Natasha is single and so am I. The time is here for me and Ms Sharon to be together.

I'm almost finished with my programme at Tabankulu. I have Natasha's number and speak to her almost every night. The plan is as follows: I'm moving into a halfway house over the next few days and we would meet for coffee the first weekend I'm free. When this weekend comes, we meet at Catura, but we decide not to stay for coffee. We go and get a DVD and go back to Natasha's house. She is wearing a small *Guess* skirt; showing off her fine legs, and a small tight shoe string vest, showing off everything else. We don't watch the movie, all I know is we are locked in each other's arms loving and kissing. I think to myself: The relationship is on.

Fall from Grace

This was the first time I was properly clean. I had stopped working my programme of recovery, and everything was centered around the relationship. I had stopped doing the required amount meetings. I also stopped talking to my sponsor. I started lying to my counsellor. I would say that I was going to a lunch time meeting and I would actually be going to Natasha's house. Natasha was asked to do some house sitting in Clifton and I went there one Saturday morning. I landed up not going back to the halfway house till Monday morning. Needless to say I began swopping the desire for drugs with earth shattering sex.

The problem with me and Natasha was we became very volatile. When we fought it was hectic, shouting, and screaming, usually followed by crazy make up sex. I got really protective and jealous about anyone she spoke to. One day I was walking through the taxi rank on my way to Natasha's house. I got offered drugs. The thought was pleasant but not worth it, so I said no thanks.

The next day, the same time, in the same place, the same dude asked me the same question. Just like that I agreed. I had about R500 on me.

The nerves when you're about to relapse after a stretch of time is intense. It usually fucks up your bowl system. My stomach hurt and I was walking with this dodgy ass homeless looking fellow into what I know now as Salt River. At the time I didn't know that Salt River is a heavy gangster area. The gangsters I knew in Oz and Jozi are very different to the Cape numbers. I believe these numbers are more disorganized but also more brutal and savage. I didn't know then that I was walking into a fucking 26's house.

We walk to a black door with a little slit. The slit in the door opens and a pair of blood shot eyes peek through and ask in a language that I don't understand: 'WHAT THE FUCK DO YOU WANT?' The dude I'm with responds and the door opens. Almost straight away I know I'm in trouble.

This place reminded me of the slums in Brazil, dodgy fucks all around. All were looking for what they could eat and the white Jewish boy from Sandton was looking rather tasty. The dude scored some crack but I wasn't interested in crack. Back in those days I was only interested in downers.

'Where is the Thai, Bro?' I asked, getting impatient and nervous at all the eyes staring at me.

'We going now to get you stuff', he said in between puffing the pipe.'

I had two or three hits and didn't get much from it. As far I was concerned, crack was rubbish.

We left the dodgy alley, and the crack house and headed towards the unknown. We arrived at a small house that was locked down like a prison. The thing about houses like this is they are usually keeping people out. Nonetheless, once you get inside, those bars and big metal doors will keep you inside.

We arrive and the scumbag starts talking to two guys. They speak loudly, making signs with their hands. One of the guys drags his finger across his throat. I know this signifies cutting someone's throat.

I'm suddenly man-handled and thrown into a room. The door is closed and the dude I was with is thrown into another room. Loud noises erupt. I'm ready to piss in my pants. The fear is gripping but I try take in my sorroundings.WHAT THE FUCK? I see a young colored-looking girl in nothing but panties sleeping on a really dirty old mattress. I stand there and look at her bare back. I wonder what her boobs look like. There's another bed and a cupboard. That's all. A guy I've never seen comes in with a "2" tattooed on his one cheek and a "6" on the other. He pushes me to the side and heads towards the cupboard. He comes out with a 13 inch screw driver and says something in Afrikaans before he leaves the room.

Fear bites me and I suddenly want to cry. What the fuck is going on? These gangsters are going to kill me! What the fuck am I going to do? How am I going to get out of here? These fucking guys are serious. I hear screaming and noises next door. The chick is still sleeping like this is normal shit around here. It probably is.

The door opens and two of them walk in. One has no shirt and is tattooed literally from head to toe. The other has a serious scar across his cheek.

Fall from Grace

They speak at me in Afrikaans. I say 'Sorry, I don't understand.' They look at each other and some words like *rooinek* are thrown around.

Then the question is repeated in English: 'What the fuck do you want here?'

'I just wanted to get some Thai Bro', I say, holding my hands up in front of me (probably because I don't know what else to do with them).

'Where's your money?', the 26 on his face asks?

'That other guy whom I came with has it.'

The non-tattooed dude runs out the room. He runs out the front door and down the road.

The scary tattooed dude points at me with the long ass rusty screw driver, and says: 'Take your clothes off.'

Fuck off. I've heard about these guys. They're going to rape me. Oh my God, now it's over. I'm going to be gang-raped by two heavy probably HIV-carrying gangsters.

'No Dude, please, just let me go, I won't say anything please.'

'Take it off now!!!', he screams at me.

Holy fuck, I'd rather die honestly than deal with this. I get the bravery and say 'I'd rather you stab me.'

'Vir wat?', he asks and then changes dialect. He switches to English: 'For what? We're not 28. We're not going to rape you, we are 26s. Just need to see that you're not wearing a wire. Are you a policeman?'

'No, I'm not.'

Nathan Daniels

'Let's see... take it off.' I strip very quickly. I'm left standing in my boxers. He pulls them down and asks me to lift my balls.

This rediculiously awkward situation is finally over. I put all my clothes on again. Now the mood changes. The guy who ran after the dodgy street cat comes back in, huffing and puffing. They speak in Afrikaans and I hear the word 400 said.

'So sit bra, relax. Now you safe, that guy was going to kill you, the finger gets dragged across the throat again.' He bumps the girl to wake her.

Secretly I giggle inside because I'm about to see her boobs. She rolls over and yep I see them. Don't fucking stare Nathan, they will probably cut you. The tattooed guy says some words I don't understand. The girl reaches into her panties, spreads her legs and takes out a long strip of crack, all in little separate packets. He says no and gives her another command. The same procedure is repeated, but this time an even longer strip of the little joined packets are pulled out of her baby maker. Don't fucking stare Nathan. Don't fucking stare. I do grab a few looks but not enough to be gutted.

'How many you want?'

'How many do you want to give me?'

'We will give you three now and we see later', he says as he lights a blunt.

The joint is passed around. We laugh and they teach me a few words in Afrikaans that I can't pronounce or remember, they even make me lunch.

Note to self: It turned out to be an awesome day but not something I would like to go through again.

Within a few weeks I'm using every day again. I find the usual Nigerians in Sea Point, so I never need to go to those gangsters again, even though they invited me back.

Now my routine is to go in the morning, meet the Nigerians, and then go to Natasha's house, while she goes to college I use in her room and then usually fall asleep.

I was staying at a halfway house called Serendipity. Let me tell you that staying in a halfway house, surrounded by recovering addicts and using drugs like heroin and crack is a terrible situation to find yourself in.

However, as they say, what doesn't come out in the wash comes out in the rinse. I was tested one night and obviously it came out positive. I was asked to leave. Now the only person I had in Cape Town was Natasha but she lived with her mom and I couldn't exactly move into their house. The night I got kicked out I stayed at her house but it was for one night only. The next night I was on the street. I had no idea how used to being on the street I would get.

As said in the beginning, I cried a lot in Cape Town. I had never thought all those years ago that from smoking a bit of weed and having a beer I would land up on the streets with nothing left. I left a bag of clothes at the halfway house and another bag at Natasha's house.

My day to day activity involved either going to Natasha's house in the morning, showering and using. I ate what I could and chilled there till she got home. We would have sex and sometimes when I was lucky I would sleep over at her house. If not I was either on a bench on the Promenade or down on the beach in a little cove. Those were my sleeping places. To score, I had a few options: Robbing people, breaking into houses, selling clothes or convincing dealers to give me credit. I would use wherever I could. Public bathrooms in Sea Point or Natasha's house were my usual places.

The life of a using addict is quite simple and predictable. We sleep, scratch, vomit or we're straight and look for ways to score. We also do a lot of waiting. Nigerians have this unbelievable ability to make junkies wait, and the more sick you're, the longer you're going to wait. That's just the way it is.

I must say that being an addict is a tiresome activity. It really does take up a lot of time and energy. Also, the behaviours we learn as we trudge the road of dark destiny get darker the further down the road we get. I never used to think

Nathan Daniels

I'd actually become a gangster or a gun or knife wielding criminal. However, as the dark descended upon my life, so did the criminal activities.

Yes I did always act as though I was hardcore. Yet, my soul is made of jelly and my exterior is not real. I'm really a soft and loving person…

One day I arrive at Natasha's house earlier than usual. I wake her. I've been using for a few days now and the sickness has started creeping in. I want her to wake up and go to college so I can use. She does the usual morning routine. I hope she doesn't want to have sex, because I won't be able to function properly. Thank God, she doesn't want to. She showers and gets dressed while I lie in bed. You see I'm very good at doing absolutely fuck-all and that's exactly what I plan on doing. She gives me a kiss and leaves.

I wait for a little and then head to the kitchen. I grab some tin foil and head back to her room and then to the bathroom. I sit on the toilet seat and prepare a hit as I light the foil. The smoke starts to rise, and I inhale. The blinds open up. Natasha is standing there.

'Nathan! What are you doing' she cries. I'm quiet. I'm caught red-handed.

And so the shit hits the proverbial fan. She leaves the room and then comes back inside. Her eyes look so upset. We scream and fight. I say 'Don't worry, I'm leaving.'

I head towards the door and she shouts 'No! No! No Nathan! don't go!

She comes up to me and hugs me. 'Please don't go' she begs me, crying.

We have some sort of fucked up sex which during she starts to cry.

I get up and put my clothes on and leave. I leave her crying on the bed, naked and torn.

I don't really feel shit. I mean I'm not a sociopath, but I think of the heroin now. I know it has this amazing ability to make one feel very little.

So I leave Natasha on the bed and I know I just want to get more fucked up.

That's exactly what I will do. I don't know how I get away with half the shit I do. I'm clearly fucked up.

Even so, I still managed to convince my family that I should stay in Cape Town and live by myself. First I found like this student house in Camps Bay and I basically turned that into a brothel and a drug house. I had prostitutes and gangsters running all over that place. I guess I was trying to extort them, or maybe the truth is that those gangsters were trying to extort me and I deflected that towards the other guys staying in the house.

One night we threw a party and I was the connection between the party people and unlimited drugs. I asked if I could invite some people and everyone agreed: 'Of course, and please bring girls'. I spoke to SKB (the main dealer in Sea Point) and he sent seven lovely looking girls. They all were fiends, thieves, and pros.

Why is it that girls extort people so much better than guys? Anyway all the girls got paid that night, and they all took some unsuspecting university boys and either robbed them blind or made an agreement that they would be paid for the service they had on offer. The drugs came at a higher price than usual, because I always took a section and then used with them anyway.

Within a few days after the party, the students got together and decided that I was to move out. Nonetheless, I had different thoughts on the Matter. When they called me in that afternoon to tell me about their decision, I proposed to them some other options. It was something like this:

I can move out and not pay you for this month's rent or I can stay and pay you. There's another option: I can get some of my boys to come over and convince you that it's in your best interest to allow me to stay here. Do you Fuckers not realise who or what I'm? Do you realise if I wanted to I could take this house over and turn it into a crack house? I could be giving the owner three times what he is getting now and have all of you looking for new residence. At this time, one of the bigger lads said that it was bullshit'. He stood up and came towards me. I had been blasting rocks for three days so I was edgy and excitable. I hit him square in the eye. In hind sight, I wish I didn't do that because, in turn, I got a savage beating from him.

What he didn't realise was that because my ego was hurt, I became very vengeful and vicious. A lot of people know that I don't let go of things very easily.

The next day I set into play a set of shattering and unsettling events.

I was chilling with SK and Sniper and told them the story of what had happened. Within fifteen minutes, myself, SK, Sniper and two other fellas where on our way up there. I must say I was bent on revenge and I was pretty drunk (probably not the best mixture to have). SK was the only one who had a weapon -- a really shiny nine millimeter.

We get to the house. I see the lights upstairs are on so I know that they're home. Or at least someone is home. We enter through my side door, and walk straight upstairs. I hear the door lock from their side. I knock and tell them to open up.

'Fuck off Nathan', is the response.

I move to the side as the one dude's foot connects with the door handle. The wood splinters all over the place. The door bursts open. I walk in slowly. The big fellow who hit me is sitting on the couch with his chick. His name is Brad.

'Where are the rest of you fagots?, I ask, while looking him in the eye.

'It's just us. Sean is sleeping.'

'Go fucking get him', I say to Sniper, 'The second door on the left!'

He storms off, and comes back with a disheveled looking man.

'So Motherfucker, you want to get brave now?', I ask, stepping closer to them.

I ask SK for his piece, and I hold the gun in Brad's face. He doesn't flinch.

'Fuck you really are a fucking hero Brad, how about this? SK take this beautiful girl. Here she's coming with us. We can sell her to those numbers who sell meth.'

SK moves towards her. She shouts out 'NO, NO, PLEASE...!'

Brad is on his feet as I thought he would be. I introduce the butt of the gun to the bridge of his nose. Blood decorates my shoes and the cream carpet.

Chaos erupts, Brad's girl is screaming and crying. I grab her and throw her on the couch. Sean takes the safe route and keeps his mouth closed. Brad wriggles on the floor as he tries to stand up. Sniper catches him on the nose again with his timberlands. The pain must be the reason why Brad loses consciousness. He lays still.

'So now I'm going to tell you what is going to happen', I say to Sean.

'Okay Nathan, I'm sorry it turned out like this. I never meant for anyone to get hurt.'

'Fuck that. It's too late for apologies.'

I look at the two gents who will remain nameless. I tell them to go through all the rooms and find bags and take anything of value. They leave straight away.

'No', says Sean. 'My computer has all my work on it, please Nathan.'

'Fuck off Sean, should have thought about all this before you guys tried to hustle me.'

Brad starts moaning softly. His girl leans next to him and speaks softly.

I grab her by the hair and pull her up. 'Brad say good bye to her because I'm taking her with me.'

He whimpers, 'Please stop, Please, I'm sorry Nathan, I'm sorry.'

'You're not really sorry Brad, but you will be.'

'The lads have finished their search and have come up with really good stuff. A few days of eating, smoking and drinking in excess is on its way.

I say to SK 'Grab her and let's get out of here.'

Screams emanate around the room again. Suddenly Brad is on his feet. Before I've got time to react I'm being tackled towards a window.

As I said in the opening of the book, I cried alot in Cape Town. I had never thought all those years ago that from smoking abit of weed and having a beer I would land up here, on the streets with nothing left, I left a bag of clothes at the halfway house and another bag at Natasha's house.

The life of a using addict is quite simple and predictable.

We sleep, scratch, vomit or we are straight and looking for ways to score.

Falling from a story onto your back with a rugby prop on top of you isn't what you would want to call a pleasurable experience.

Memorable, but pleasurable most definitely not. We hit the ground or bushy shrubbery kind of on our sides. My biggest fear was that, there were pieces of glass under me and they went into my body on impact.

For a few minutes I couldn't really feel anything. The shock and horror of the decision Brad had made was still running around my mind. Could this be real, did I just get tackled through a fucking window? The reality is I was just tackled through a window and I wasn't in great shape. By the looks of it, neither was Brad. He lay very still in a muddled heap on the floor. Do I dare move or should I wait for fuck knows what to happen? I better try to get up then. I try sit up and the inevitable happens -- pain like burning hot knives rips through my lower back. If I move again I might just pass out. I try one more movement and everything fades to black.

When I come by, I'm lying on the couch downstairs in our house. There's no-one around. At this moment I realise just how alone I actually am. No mother to look after my wounds. Natasha is busy at college. When I think back I remember thinking I could've died and no-one would've even known till my body started smelling. I think about the life I used to have and how I miss that so much right now. I wish I was happy and with people who really loved me. I think of how perfect my life was before Australia. I wish my life would be happy like that again. The drugs have killed a lot more than my family and brain cells.

I decide to stand and check where my phone is. I need to call my mom. Hopefully she will give me another chance to get my shit together. What baffles me is this isn't the first time I've had this realization. In the past, there has been a genuine desire to stop using. So many times I would throw away my stash and swear to myself and to God that it's now over. The next morning I would be in the huge garbage bin at the back of my house again sifting through week-old garbage, smelling so bad that I would often gag, looking for any trace of the gear or of something that I might have thrown away during the week. I would often swear and carry on like a fool for being so weak and desperate.

I try phone my mom and it goes straight to voice mail. I hobble to my room. It takes me almost five minutes to get there. Usually it would have taken me about five to ten seconds only.

I gently lower myself on the bed and pain shoots through me again. Perhaps I broke my ass bone or maybe something worse? I reckon I should probably go to the hospital but I don't have the energy really and I can't ask Natasha because she doesn't have a car or a license. The option to call her mom is a definite NO, NO.

What I do is, get into bed. I pull the covers over my battered and bruised body and for two days that's where I stay.

Nathan Daniels

I went to rehab back in Jozi after a whole fall out with SK and Sniper. I had moved into a B and B and also had a fall out with the owner. Natasha and I were over, we just didn't know it yet. We went back and forth with each other till I left and went to rehab in Plett. From Plett the decision was that I was going to move back to Australia to live with Dad and his new crew. I was pretty pleased with it because I would have a break from South Africa. This would also give my mom some breathing space because this whole process has taken its toll on her. I don't think you could imagine what it must have been like for her. What that dear women has gone through. Honestly, I'm surprised that she is still alive. I believe that in life God gives people guardian angels. I know for sure that Fiona Lancaster is mine. She has kept me alive countless times. Through it all, I never realized just how special of a women my beautiful mom is.

So back to the land of the sheep shaggers for me. I always thought that it was a just a saying "sheep shager" until the day I met Mathew in a rehab. The rehab was out in a small town called Orange, a very, very country town. If you put two and two together, you'll get my drift. Mathew, small town and sheep!

It was a very strange moment when Mathew decided to tell me about growing up on a farm. All those things came in the distance waving at me, once I had got in ear shot.

'Nathan, this is Melissa, Melissa this is my son Nathan'.

I see my dad and his new Mrs....

Chapter 17

Being a hustler on the streets of Sydney Australia isn't joyous at all. I just signed up for disability payments, You see the great Australian government worked out this awesome plan for us drug addicts. They pump the system full of tax payers' money, and then drug addicts like myself apply for a disability because we're unfit to work. Then we get payments every fortnight for sitting on our stoned asses doing sweet fuck-all. It's a good deal as long as it's enough to keep junkies off the street stealing and causing trouble.

My dream of living out of home with a friend had finally come true. I could use as much as I wanted and do whatever I wanted. I would drink first thing in the morning coupled with a few breakfast bongs. Then the hustle started -- where to get some meth, junk or anything that would send me on my way to oblivion. And so the story begins.

'Yo what's up Bro?' I ask Luke rolling on my thin bed of two blankets on an even thinner carpet. No mattress here, I'm slumming it.

Luke rolls over; he looks sick as well as hungry.

While I roll a smoke, I ask, 'Dude you want a smoke?'

He mumbles a no and turns over, attempting to fall asleep again.

'Oh shit Dude, you know what day it is?' I say again, trying to jolt my good friend awake.

He rolls over and says 'It's Wednesday.' 'No dumb ass, it's my pay day.'

Luke sits up quickly, realizing the immensity of this situation.

'You right Dude, here.'

He throws me the phone and tells me to call Eugene.

I do so. Two coffees and a couple of bongs and drinks later, Eugene arrives with a fat gram of crystal for us. Once again, I need a shit the minute I see the ice. But I don't trust anyone around the goods so I sit and begin the process of smoking a first very fat hit. As I exhale the massive cloud of smoke out my nose, I spin. My head is numb and my body is seriously going through orgasms, got to love meth.

The mental suicide that I constantly go through starts fading away, and my troubled mind calms down. It is replaced by a different manifested thought, which is 'don't fucking trust anyone, especially that dodgey Russian Eugene'. We all know he taxed some one the way over here. So he doesn't deserve to smoke any. But he will, he will have a hit or two.

The release I feel every time I put a chemical into my system never disappoints me. The closer I get to oblivion, the better.

Note to self: The days of using drugs for pleasure are long gone.

The longer I stay away from reality, the harder and darker reality seems: Small everyday problems are fucking

impossible to deal with. I can't function like Luke or Dom. How the fuck can they go to gym and university and focus on what they doing?... cos I find it impossible to think of anything else except using.

Oblivion comes fast on this grade a drug: Life's menial problems fade in an instant.

Luke's phone rings while he is in the shower, I answer.

'What the fuck is up brother?', I ask one of our clients.

'Yeah, hold up I'll let you in', I say in true hustler style.

I make my way up the broken carpet to the front door. I peer through the keyhole as Luke always does. I wouldn't want to get done over like some of the other hustlers we know. They got sloppy, but I won't get sloppy.

I open the door. 'Whats happening Dude?' I ask, putting out my hand in the way us boys who grew up on Bondi always do.

Our client puts his hand in mine and we embrace with one hand around each other's backs.

'Not much Bro, just looking for something to smoke. You holding?'

'You know bra, we always got the hook up', I say while closing the door and returning back to the smoke den.

We enter the room and our client spots the meth pipe and says, 'Oh shit Dude, let me hit that.'

'You got four clips Dude?', I ask, not wanting to share with the scab.

'No Bro, but...'

'No buts... it costs 400 and there's no ticking up.'

I move over to the cupboard, take out the coffee tin filled with stinky, stinky bud.

'How much you want bro?' I ask, now sitting on the couch and taking a massive hit of the meth.

He stares at the pipe, drooling, and then says 'Just a stick, Dude.'

I take out the scales and weigh up a stick. As I'm doing this, Luke walks in.

'Shit you, Fuckers gave me a fright', he says with goose pimples all over his body.

'Sorry, what's up Yayo', our client asks..

'Fuck-all Bro. What you getting?'

'Just a wicko Bro, got to go to school.'

Luke picks up the meth pipe and has a huge hit. Smoke billows out his nose. His eyes roll and close. I can relate to that feeling and I want it now. I stick out my hand; he hands me the glass pipe. I repeat what Luke has just done and my eyes roll and close. Lick lips, lick lips.

'Sweet boys I'm out', our client says, handing over the twenty to Luke.

I stand and say good bye to our loyal client, and then put the weed back in its rightful place.

The door closes and we go back to our usual routine. Luke obsessively cuts up his Source and XXL magazines sticking pictures all over one of the walls. I'll admit that it looks fucking sick though.

I start graffing. I play music on my ultimate obsession play station. I've been jamming Scarface for weeks now. I fucking love this shit.

I fall into a horrible thought process. The years of drug abuse have taken their toll. I grab the meth and tell Luke I'm going to get some grog and some smokes for us.

I don't trust him with the meth. I don't trust anyone including myself with this shit. I've seen many people go fucking nuts from this shit. People kill other each other over this shit more than any other drugs. Well, maybe not crack.

I walk out the place in a weird psycho trance. I'm fixated on Luke who is using all my meth while I'm gone. I know he has already taxed some so he can smoke that.

Fall from Grace

As I walk into the street, the scorching Sydney sun fills my face, and my eyes start to hurt from the glare.

I feel my sanity slipping away. I need more... a lot more. I need heroin, meth, rocks, pills, and alcohol.

This is unfair. Where the fuck am I going to find the cash? I'm fucking sick of this small time using. I want, no I NEED a binge. What can I steal? Or more appropriate, WHO can I steal from? As I'm walking, my dad calls. I choose not to answer his call. He gives a fuck anyway.

Maybe I can rob his new family -- his new fucking family; there are computers, laptops, phones, jewels, and many other goodies, I suspect. They will know straight away that it was me -- so that rules out the new family. Maybe I can break into someone's house. I look at every house I walk past, what about that one or that one, I ask myself.

Well, I've got enough money to get a fifth of vodka. So that's what I'll do, I'll have a fat line of meth, then drink the whole bottle before I get back. How else can I get fucked up? I have not had sex in ages. I need to fuck, I should pay a trip to a pro in the cross again. I love the *no strings attached* sex in a dirty alley. Fuck, its so good.

Clarity, look where my life is. I've not eaten a meal in like four days. I've slept very uncomfortably for the past few weeks. I'm sitting here thinking of fucking whores, I'm thinking of robbing everyone I know and digging this hole deeper. What has happend to me and how do I get out of this place? The idea is, I blow out heavily on the goods and land up in rehab again.

So that's the plan. Now the question. Where to get the money for a significant binge? It would cost around $3000 I reckon.'

I've got a plan.

Chapter 18

Myself and three other friends are in a skiing store. We are acting suspicious as hell. Friend one came up with a plan, and we're actually going through with it.

I try on a ski mask and it fits well. I look mean as hell. Friends one and two do the same. We go up to the counter and a weird old man looks at the three ski masks, then looks at us, and then asks, 'You boys going skiing?'

Friend one says, 'Yeah we're going to Sweden Tomorrow, just getting last minute things.'

The clerk's wife hears us and says, 'Oh that's lovely. You boys enjoy.'

'We will, thank you', friend two says.

We walk out. I got fucking huge butterflies about this plan, but the urge to binge is finally coming to an end. Oblivion is around the corner. Yip de fucking do.

Next stop on our travels is a tool store.

We enter and walk straight over to our weapons of choice: I pick up a massive fucking panga. Oh yes, I don't even need to look around anymore this is it!

Friend two takes an over-sized crowbar, and friend one also falls to the trend of the big fuck off panga.

We are now set to do out job.

One thing left, we got to wait for nightfall. Friend three will be the get away driver. The rest of the day is spent relaxing, smoking bud, having a few drinks and running over the plans in our heads.

The sun sets at the end of this spectacular day.

Friend three knocks on the door. I open and greet him. I need to vomit I'm so nervous.

We round up the goods, ski masks, panga black clothes. I mean, I really look the part, black hoodie, black shorts, and black ski mask, not to mention black panga.

The drive is agonising, I truly might vomit. I've never done a proper job before, and the boys know this.

They sit in silence, while friend one tries to locate the house, he spots it. Friend one jumps out the car to go assess the situation. We stop outside. Friend one returns and says 'It's on boys'. I hand out the masks, I place my mask over my head and my hoodie over that. I have ready my panga and step out the car. Friend one and two rush towards the front door. This idiot left it open, he deserves what's coming.

We enter the house, and friend one immediately points us in the direction of this idiot's room. He then runs off into another room to begin the search.

Friend two and I head into the back room, where our victim sits and waits.

He thinks it's a joke at first, probably some of his friends fucking around, but sadly for him it;s not to be. Friend two is silent, so I better say something: 'This isn't a joke Motherfucker, you make any sudden moves or noise and I will drive this panga into your skull', I say mustering up as much gangsterism as I can.

His smile dissipates instantly as he realises this is not a joke. He realises that we're not his friends and we're here to take all his shit.

'Okay, okay, I won't do anything', he says and slowly pushes his computer chair back, while Scrubs plays on his computer.

'Where the fuck is the drugs?' Friend two asks moving towards the fag.

'In...in.. in the TV room… the bag with a shoe-box in it.'

I turn and enter the room with the TV and locate the bag. Friend two brings the poof out into the lounge.

I open the bag, and remove the box. Inside lies a treasure chest of goodies: 500 small green pills, a couple of small bags of coke and ketimine. A small bundle of money. Nothing significant though.

Friend one comes out the darkness of the other room with a bag full of goodies. He can't speak in front of our victim because our victim might know his voice. So he comes closer to me and says 'SAFE.'

How could I forget? The safe!

'Where's the safe Motherfucker? Answer me wrong once and your fingers are gone.'

The victim falls silent. Fuck it's not him who is a victim, I am the victim. He sells drugs to people like me.

Friend one kicks him very hard in the ribs. He falls off the couch and says 'Okay.'

'It's in the room…' He is now crying 'It's in the room.'

Friend two moves the idiot into the room. I watch him while friend two hits and beats on him: 'What is the code?' he repeats over and over.

The dealer surrenders the code, Friend two keys in the code and then the satisfying sound of a lock unlocking, breaks the silence.

'Okay, there's $15000 in there. Take it and get the fuck out of here.'

'You're swearing at us now?' I ask. 'You see this is our area, we deal in here, we run the show. If we hear you've been dealing again, we'll be back to finish you off. You understand, Motherfucker?'

'Yes...yes now go. Just for good measure, Friend two swings and catches him square in the jaw with the back of the panda handle. The stupid, now broke Motherfucker falls onto his bed, with his eyes closed. No squealing, no noise. Our chance to escape.

I pick up the backpack full of money and drugs and we head off to the front door, closely followed by Friend one. 'You get the cash?'

'Yeah Bro, we got $15000 and a whole bunch of goodies.'

'Sweet, let's get the fuck out of here, where is Friend two?'

'Don't know… he's coming now. Let's go.'

Friend one runs back to find Friend two.

I'm first out of the door. The mask comes off and so does the hoodie. I run down the street to find Friend three and the car.

He sits, waiting for us.

I jump in the back seat.

'So what's going on? Where is everyone else?' Friend Three asks.

I look down the street to see Friend one and two running towards the car.

They jump in. Friend three starts the car and drives off. We all slap hands, laugh and joke about how scared that bitch was. I feel good, I got at least $5000 in my pocket for this little job. Oblivion is on its way.

The money is settled. I take the $4000 cash into my hands. Friend one says, 'I can't believe I'm giving Nathan this much money.'

Everyone in the room agrees.

I laugh while sniffing the remainder of the blow. It's shit quality and it burns my nose.

They have no idea what's about to go down.

I get home after the job and ask Luke if he wants to get some meth. 'Yeah man, I phones Eugene.'

'Dude, Eugene's got none; he reckons the East coast is dry', Luke says looking really disappointed.

'What about some coke? I can get prime blow' Luke says again.

'Yeah, sweet Bro, make the call', I say, counting my money again.

We order a delivery of a bottle of whiskey and an eight ball of so called good blow.

Mr Delivery arrives and comes in, the deal is done. The plate is put in the microwave followed by the coke poured onto the heated surface of the fake china.

I drop an E and a sleeping pill, have a shot or two and begin to snort massive lines of the blow.

Soon we find out its the shittest quality blow we have ever done. I laugh and drop my second pinger. The first one has kicked in and the sleeping pill is counter acting its effect. The alcohol is just there cos I love it, the

Fall from Grace

blow isn't even worth making lines, we just dip our fingers in the blow and snort straight off our hands.

Now is the profound part. For the next ten days, I have three memories:

The first memory is of Luke's older brother, knocking on the door. The story behind this, is that Luke's brother Ben is not allowed to know we're using so I go into a paranoid panic, closing all the curtains. Running around, hand in the blow, sniff sniff, lie on the floor, look out under the door, and then the curtain again, hand, blow, sniff, and sniff. This goes on for twenty minutes, thoroughly scaring one of our clients. All I hear is him saying 'I need to get out of here.' I tackle him on the floor. 'No Dude, you can't, relax, stop freaking out.' Then my mind goes blank again.

The next memory is of me and Luke, talking to a pro in the cross about getting us smack. She leaves her bag with us and heads off to get us a decent gram of china white.

This memory ties in with being back in the flat using the heroin.

The last memory I have is still very lucid. Luke has told Ben that I've lost my mind. I'm standing in the flat, screaming that I need more ice or heroin. I can't remember what drug I wanted. I just knew I wanted more. Then I woke up in hospital with a big problem. Apparently my kidneys were shutting down.

The doctor asks me what I've used. I list off all the drugs I've used.

He misunderstands me. 'No, young man, what have you used in the last few days?'

I list the drugs again, 'heroin, base, coke, special K, vodka, ecstasy, stilnox, tranq's and weed.'

He looks at the nurse and walks off to talk to her.

Nathan Daniels

He returns. I wither in pain. My stomach hurts as well as my lower back. I can't urinate or move.

My father sits at my side. I'm not sure how long he sits there, but I feel it's a long time.

I overhear the doctor telling my dad, that I might not make it. I've consumed enough drugs to kill a full grown adult. They get my blood results back, and the doctor comes up to me and calls me a miracle.

'Nathan, you shouldn't be alive, your system is totally wrecked. We have no other choice than to commit you, which means for a week you will be under 24 hour supervision. Also, we're going to put you to sleep for a day or two, to stop the delusions you're having. Are you okay with that?'

I mumble out a sentence that has nothing to do with his question, 'Yeah, two grams will be great.'

The doctor nods and says 'I'll come see you Tomorrow, I'm very worried about your toxicity levels.

I try work out where I'm and what's going on.

Note to self: Nothing really comes to surface.

My mind can't tell the difference between reality and fantasy, a fantasy that I've created.

I'm constantly seeing weird people come up to take my blood pressure. I keep thinking they're aliens, or worse, vampires.

Every move I make reminds me I'm lying on sharp shards of glass. Each shard of glass stabs into my soft skin.

I fall into a two day long sleep with the help of Valium -- an old friend.

Good night God, I say to a nurse walking by.

Chapter 19

Eventually I come by in the hospital. My surroundings are slowly going back to normal. There is an old man named Julius who has given up his nights to do volunteer work. I'm committed to old Julius. He is my caretaker and he gets me something to drink when I need a drink. He gets me a Valium when I ask him for a Valium.

He talks to me, knowing exactly what I am, and what I do. I smell really bad. I haven't showered for at least three weeks. For the first time in a week I ask to go to the toilet. Trusty old Julius stands at the door, while I scream at the pain and horror of seeing thick dry blood passing through my urine. The doctor must have warned him of what was to come, cos as I walk out he says, 'Nathan, would you like a cigarette now?'

A fucking smoke. 'I would love one, old chap.' I say in a very excited tone.

Julius smiles a smile of compassion and understanding. 'Let's go', Julius says.

He hands me a personal favorite, a Winfield blue.

I take the smoke and put it in my cracked, broken lips and spark.

The smoke stalks around me. I inhale and it burns. I exhale it burns. After the third or forth drag, my head spins and spins. It's that feeling that I've longed for. I no longer want to feel anything remotely close to heroin or the warm burning sensation of 101 over proof rum running down my throat. All I want now is to feel something, something humane, something real.

I tell my caretaker that I'm done, my innings are over. I've lived the life I wanted to live and I got nothing except pain and disaster from it. I tell him cos he'll believe me. My family won't believe me anymore, they've heard it way too many times.

My dad comes to visit and brings clothes that aren't three weeks old, or crusty and smelly.

I have the first shower I've had in weeks. Something in my mind is different. There's a new feeling. Maybe not new, but just old and forgotten. I feel unbelievable when I got new clothes on. My father tells me I'm going to Sydney Clinic again. This time I'm under strict supervision. Still committed you know, except it's not 24 hour supervision. This time it's every hour they tick my name off on a list.

I smile, hug my dad and thank him for his help. I see the look of desperation in his eyes. He almost lost me for good this time. It hurts to see his blue eyes. The pain he experiences is far different to mine. I wouldn't know where to begin with a son like myself. You've done well Dad, you've done well.

I say my goodbyes to my fair old Julius. I'm going to miss his compassion and weird sort of humour. 'Old chap, thanks for all your care and support', I want to hug him but I don't. Instead, I turn my back and walk out with my father, off to Sydney clinic I go.

I get out the only piece of luxury I've been in for months, my dad's beautiful Merc. I've got no belongings with me.

So we go straight into my next resting place for the next three months.

I'm admitted by the same weird Irish woman who admitted me when I was young. She asks, 'So young man, are you ready now?

'Yes I am. God's honest truth, I am', I say, truly believing and meaning my words.

Fall from Grace

She tells us to go up to Level 2, the drug addicts' ward. I know this place. I know the nurses. The rooms are luxurious, we got a TV in our room, our own bathrooms and of course, an essential in Sydney, a summer air con.

Surprising for rehabs but the beds are seriously comfortable. I flop onto my bed and fall asleep within seconds.

I feel my dad put the blanket over my worn body. He kisses my head and tells me he'll see me Tomorrow.

I thank him with a pre-sleep mumble after which I fall deep deep into a dream of sorts. I'm free of the chains of this endless addiction. I've got my family back together and my life is in order. I'm a successful writer and a counselor for young kids who are going through exactly what I went through. Most importantly, I'm happy, real happy, happy without drugs. It's a very different happiness because it's from within.

Sadly, I'm woken by a lovely nurse. Funny enough she's from South Africa. She's an African woman with big black cascading hair and a milk chocolate skin. I love her the minute I see her. She is officially my new best friend.

'Sorry my Boy, I got to take your blood pressure.'

I willingly hand over my arm and she takes my pressure and says its high. My palms sweat, and my body still aches. I feel like I need to use. I really don't want to, but my body is saying something else.

COME ON PUSSY GO USE, SWEET SWEET HEROIN, GET SOME BEAUTIFUL METH INTO YOURSELF, OKAY JUST WEED NATHAN, JUST A SIMPLE LITTLE JOINT.

'Pesh, my body feels like it wants to use.'

'Okay my darling, come with me to the nurses' station, she says lovingly, like a true women of Africa.

I try stand but Im still quite weak. My legs feel like jelly. Pesh helps me to stand and then assists me to the station. She goes into the meds room, opens

the little meds window and hands me two Valiums. I take them and following procedure, I show her my mouth is empty.

'Thanks Pesh, I'm going for a smoke then I'll go back to bed. Hopefully these will let me sleep right through till Tomorrow.'

'No, you can't sleep till Tomorrow; you got to see the doctor. Sam's coming to see you. He thought you were going to die. He's the one who organised you to come here. He has already prescribed your med's.'

'Cool, Sam's a legend, what did he prescribe?'

'You got a variety of meds he wants to try you on.'

'Stilnox to sleep. Subutex for a maintenance programme. Naltrexone for prevention. Antibuse for prevention. Seroquel for moods, and Efexor for depression. Oh yeah, and Valium as PRN.

So, young man, you're sorted for a while, now go smoke, and then relax.'

'Will do lovely lady, bye', I say, feeling confident about my stay, my frame of mind and my future.

Time in rehab goes very slowly. The only good thing is the food is good. We have gourmet meals. Three courses. Love it.

Also these places are frequented by hot girls.

My days are okay here. Dr Sam Roberts has changed me from Subutex to Methadone. It makes me fucking tired to start, but eventually it settles down and I begin to feel hopeful again. After a month we start to get privileges. I'm aloud to go out for an hour a day, to get exercise. So I go down to the beach, I have a swim and I spend alot of time thinking about what I want. I really wish I could go back to South Africa, but my mom now has a new man. My sister also has a new man and she has moved to America. I'm left alone. My dad has a nice new family. I'm left alone.

There's light at the end of the tunnel. I just don't know which way the tunnel faces anymore. I can't live here; the streets of Sydney will kill me. I can't go back to South Africa, cos mom has a new life with someone and she won't take me in. They live together, so I wouldn't be able to live with them even if I wanted to.

Note to self: I couldn't live alone, I'm way to unstable.

I have no direction, I'm losing the will to stay clean. The future seems bleak, and my life force is slipping. Obviously this doesn't happen in one thought, it's rather the build-up of days and days of depressing thoughts taking their toll.

I fall into a deep depression. I go see secondary facilities and halfway houses. They are my only option, for I'm a street kid, an abandoned junkie adoptee, rejected at birth and rejected now.

There's a solution. I go get a shitty flat in the junction. I get a fat needle, I load the needle full of heroin, I hit my jugular with precision. Slowly I fade into oblivion, life slips away. I die.

'Hi Boy', my mom says, not having seen me in a long time.

She has come to visit me, how sweet.

'Hi mom', I say as I get up to hug her.

We embrace and I feel her pain. I couldn't begin to imagine what it must feel like to take on the responsibility of a child and have that child fail time after time at everything, a child who destroys his own life. For a mother to sit and watch her child die must be the worst thing in this world. 'I'm sorry mom.'

We hang out for a couple of days before she goes back.

She tells me I can't possibly come back to South Africa, she doesn't live in her own house, and there's nowhere for me to stay. We fight about stupid things. I'm ultra depressed, the Subutex is toxic in my system. I take the rejection badly and say horrible things in the process. She leaves. We are not on good terms.

The time has come… Death is around the corner. All these fucking years of pain and glory are going to end. Five days till my next Centre Link payment. That's the day. Fuck the flat. I'll go to where I belong. I'll go where this all started.

I'll climb the cliffs and sit on the edge of the rocks. I'll prepare a fix, a big fuck-off horse needle. I'll fill it with five hundred dollars worth of A grade smack and I'll bang it into my jugular. Then I'll sit and watch the world fade into oblivion, that oblivion I've been chasing for so long. I'll go to Bondi…

Epilogue

I'm jolted back to that time where it seemed the world wasn't worth living in. That time when hearts broke and opiates soothed pain:

Shouts of agony echoing into eternity. Lost dreams, hopes and goals remind me I'm a failure. She said it and she meant it: 'You're a loser and an asshole...' I feel the rage and hopelessness escaping her eyes. Her energy is dark, Charles Manson dark.

Where to from here? Obliterate my soul with more heroin? Go back to Serenity to get clean? Do I really want to clean up? The answer is, probably not.

Decisions don't last; the darkness always creeps back in and changes things. Darkness lies and tells me it'll be okay. Darkness makes everything seem light and comfortable. Darkness lies and tells me one more time we will be okay together, and things will be different.

Today I sit here... The steam from my espresso smells like the Colombian mountains before it dissipates into the atmosphere.

Three and a half years without the gear and things are better I guess. Not easy, but better.

I guess no one told me it would be easier. The darkness still lurks, awaiting its prey. Around every corner I see him, trying desperately to lure me back to destruction.

Today I make the deliberate choice to not believe those lies. Today I deal with life as it com